MEDITERRANEAN DIET COOKBOOK FOR BEGINNERS

The Complete Guide with 1000 Days of Quick & Easy Recipes in Alphabetic Order with a 7-Day Flexible Meal Plan for a Healthier Lifestyle

Stacy Haves

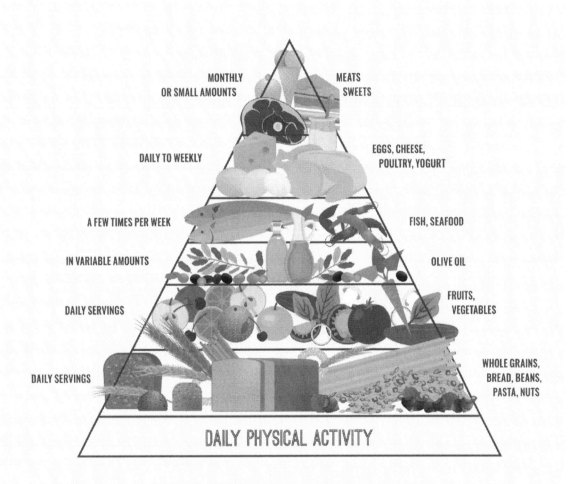

MONTHLY OR SMALL AMOUNTS — MEATS SWEETS

DAILY TO WEEKLY — EGGS, CHEESE, POULTRY, YOGURT

A FEW TIMES PER WEEK — FISH, SEAFOOD

IN VARIABLE AMOUNTS — OLIVE OIL

DAILY SERVINGS — FRUITS, VEGETABLES

DAILY SERVINGS — WHOLE GRAINS, BREAD, BEANS, PASTA, NUTS

DAILY PHYSICAL ACTIVITY

MEDITERRANEAN DIET

Table of Content

INTRODUCTION

The Mediterranean Diet is more than a set of recommended ingredients and food products. It is an authentic lifestyle based on the good habits derived from the eating traditions of the countries bordering the Mediterranean.

The Mediterranean Diet was studied and systematized by an American scholar. In the early 1950s, the American biologist Ancel Keys analysed the diet of the people of the Mediterranean basin and compared it with that of other countries. He observed the dietary habits and lifestyles of seven countries (the United States, Finland, the Netherlands, Italy, Greece, Japan, and the former Yugoslavia) to understand their effects on the population's well-being, focusing on the incidence of cardiovascular disease.

Keys' research demonstrated that a dietary style based on the consumption of grains, vegetables, fruit, fish and olive oil was undoubtedly the best alternative to traditional American and North European diets, which were too rich in fat, and animal protein and sugar.

The Mediterranean Diet is based on a series of items to be consumed daily in well-defined proportions to achieve a balanced diet that includes all macronutrients, distributed roughly according to the following breakdown: 60% carbohydrates, 25-30% fat, 10-15% protein. The main ingredients of this diet are fruits and vegetables, whole grains, olive oil, wine, fish (primarily blue), white meat, dairy products, and eggs.

Today the Mediterranean Diet has become a UNESCO World Heritage Site as an intangible asset of humanity. The Mediterranean Diet Food Pyramid illustrates the quantity and frequency of foods to eat during the day.

WHAT'S ON YOUR PLATE:

How To Combine Foods (Cal.) / How To Create Meals

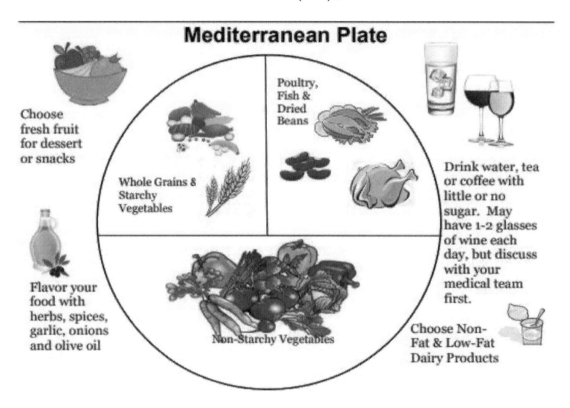

Mediterranean Plate

Choose fresh fruit for dessert or snacks

Whole Grains & Starchy Vegetables

Poultry, Fish & Dried Beans

Drink water, tea or coffee with little or no sugar. May have 1-2 glasses of wine each day, but discuss with your medical team first.

Flavor your food with herbs, spices, garlic, onions and olive oil

Non-Starchy Vegetables

Choose Non-Fat & Low-Fat Dairy Products

Mediterranean Diet Meal Plan

Food/Food Group	Recommended Intake*	Tips
Vegetables	4 or more servings each day (one portion each day should be raw vegetables)	A serving is 1 cup raw or ½ cup cooked vegetables. Eat a variety of colors and textures.
Fruits	3 or more servings each day	Make fruit your dessert
Grains	4 or more servings each day	Choose mostly whole grains. 1 serving = 1 slice bread or ½ cup cooked oatmeal
Fats/Oils	Olive Oil: 4 Tablespoons or more each day	Choose extra virgin olive oil (EVOO) and use in salad dressings and cooking; choose avocado or natural peanut butter instead of butter or margarine
Dried Beans/Nuts/Seeds	Nuts/Seeds: 3 or more servings each week Beans/Legumes: 3 or more servings each week	1 ounce or 1 serving = 23 almonds or 14 walnut halves; 1 serving of beans = ½ cup
Fish and Seafood	2-3 times each week	Choose salmon, sardines, and tuna which are rich in Omega-3 fatty acids
Herbs and Spices	Use daily	Season foods with herbs, garlic, onions and spices instead of salt
Yogurt/Cheese/Egg Poultry	Choose daily to weekly	Choose low-fat yogurt and cheeses; choose skinless chicken or turkey in place of red meat
Alcohol/Wine	Men: 1-2 glasses each day Women: 1 glass each day	Always ask your medical team if alcohol is ok for you to consume.

*Serving sizes should be individualized to meet energy and nutrient needs.
❖ Red meats, processed meats, and sweets should be limited

Example of a 7-Day Meal Plan

	BREAKFAST	LUNCH	DINNER
MONDAY	Fruity Nutty Muesli (pg 20)	Slashed Beet and Arugula Salad (pg 33)	Spicy Turkey Breast with Fruit Chutney (pg 59)
TUESDAY	Morning Couscous (pg 22)	Tuna Salad with Toasted Pine Nuts (pg 35)	Minestrone Soup (pg 44)
WEDNESDAY	Energizing Breakfast Protein Bars (pg 19)	Chickpea and Lentil Bean Soup (pg 40)	Moroccan Couscous (pg 106)
THURSDAY	Homemade Greek Yogurt (pg 21)	Slashed Beet and Arugula Salad (pg 33)	Chicken with Roasted Vegetables (pg 53)
FRIDAY	Breakfast Couscous (pg 16)	Macedonia Serving Mixed Green (pg 31)	Mediterranean Cod (pg 68)
SATURDAY	Almond Mascarpone Dumplings (pg 15)	Potato Salad with Lemon (pg 32)	Meatballs with Mushrooms (pg 79)

Follow These Tips To Adopt A Mediterranean Diet

❖ **Include fresh produce in your daily diet:** These foods should be consumed at most meals because they contain necessary nutrients such as fiber, vitamins, minerals, antioxidants, and physicochemicals. Including fresh produce in your diet can help you maintain a healthy weight and improve your overall health. Eat fresh fruit in its whole form for breakfast and snacks, and reserve fruit salad or berries for dessert; daily consumption of 100 percent fruit juice should be limited to a half cup. Make sure to eat at least one serving of vegetables at lunch, such as a spinach salad, shredded raw carrots or beets in a sandwich, red pepper sticks, or vegetable soup, and make it a goal to consume the amount of vegetables that is advised for an adult to consume on a daily basis.

❖ **Always choose for the whole grains:** As a result of the low level of processing required for these grains, barley, bulgur, couscous, rice, pasta, polenta, farro, quinoa, millet, and oats are all considered to be mainstays in the Mediterranean diet. Select cereals and bread that are created with whole grains in their whole. White rice should be had less often than brown rice and whole-grain pasta should be consumed more frequently.

❖ **Consume dairy products that are low in fat:** These foods are a good source of many nutrients, including protein, calcium, and vitamin B. Pick yogurt that is nonfat, low-fat (containing 1% milk fat), or Greek. Cheese should be used in moderation, and efforts should be made to locate skim or low-fat kinds.

❖ **Eat fish twice weekly:** At least twice each week, people should be eating fish. Every week, you should aim to consume two meals of oil-only fish in order to acquire enough of the omega-3 fats that are good for your heart. There are many delicious selections available, including salmon, sardines, herring, and trout. Fish prepared in any of these three ways (baked, broiled or steamed) is mouthwateringly good.

❖ **Reduce your consumption of red meat:** A diet that is more Mediterranean could allow for the consumption of small amounts of lean red meat (no more than 12 to 16 ounces per month). For a large steak, prefer small portions of meat in a sauté, a dish made up of meat and pasta or a stew accompanied by vegetables. Since your main course should include a 3-ounce serving, that means only half of your plate will be meat.

❖ **Include alternatives suitable for vegetarians:** You may boost the amount of protein you consume by eating at least one meal each week that is composed entirely of legumes. There are many delicious alternatives available, including pasta with white kidney beans, lentil soup, vegetarian chili, and black bean tacos.

❖ **Make smart choices when it comes to fats:** the majority of the fats you consume should be monounsaturated. Olive oil is a versatile cooking and baking ingredient. (Extra-virgin olive oil is not the best choice to use in high-temperature cooking processes like deep-frying.) Add a handful of nuts, such as almonds, pecans, and cashews, in your daily diet. Nuts are full of healthy fats and protein. While making sandwiches, you may use sliced avocado as an alternative to butter or mayonnaise.

❖ **Moderate use of alcohol:** Mediterranean Wine is often considered part of a healthy diet and is enjoyable when used in moderation with meals. This translates to a maximum of 10 ounces per day for males and five ounces per day for women. A person's taste in wine may vary, but drinking alcohol, even in moderation, may not be beneficial to their health.

A Practical Guide to The Mediterranean Diet Food Pyramid

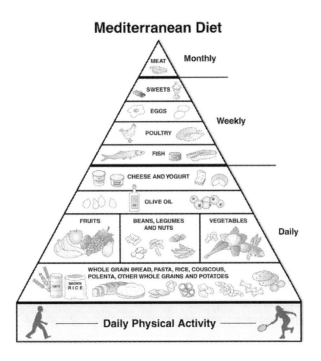

Find Out How to Make the Most of the Mediterranean Diet Food Pyramid: is based on the eating patterns of the Mediterranean's inhabitants who live the longest. A broad guideline for the food pyramid is followed, and it promotes dining together with others and leading an active lifestyle (rather than specific quantities).

Learning About The Mediterranean Diet

❖ **Plant-based diet:** The basis of your meals should contain fresh and organic fruits, vegetables, legumes, nuts, and beans. Whole foods may include considerable amounts of fiber, complex carbohydrates, antioxidants, vitamins, and minerals, all of which are helpful to your health to varied degrees. Thanks to the high fiber content of this meal, you will be less prone to eat unhealthy foods, and it will also give you with nutrients that fight sickness.

❖ **Only whole grains:** It is better to avoid refined grain products such as white rice and bleached white flour, stripped of most of their healthful nutrients. Instead, prefer wholegrain products such as oats, brown rice, whole wheat, bulgur, farro, barley, quinoa, millet corn, and so on. Whole grains are higher in fiber, minerals, and vitamins.

❖ **Fish or shellfish at least twice a week:** Low in saturated fat and a rich source of omega-3 fatty acids, fish and shellfish are a healthy choice. Fish and shellfish like as clams, anchovies, salmon, mussels, octopus, sardines, shrimp, herring, crab, squid, sardines, tuna, sea bass, and tuna are staples in the diets of individuals who practice the Mediterranean cuisine. But if you want to avoid the mercury contamination that is common in farmed fish, you should only consume fish that has been caught in the wild.

❖ **Small portions of red meat every once in a while:** Red meat may have a high level of saturated fat. While it is included in the Mediterranean diet for the health benefits it provides, it is nevertheless recommended that you consume it in moderation. You should limit your dairy intake to cheese and yogurt and eat as little dairy as possible. Both cheese and natural yogurt are staples of the Mediterranean diet due to their high protein content and low fat content when consumed in moderation. They're a good source of calcium, which is essential for strong bones. Probiotics, which yogurt is loaded with, help digestion by boosting the gut's good bacteria count.

❖ **Get healthy fats from olives, avocado, fatty fish, nuts, seeds, and olive oil:** Olives and olive oil, in general, are rich in monounsaturated fats and antioxidants that promote heart health. Eat olives as a snack or add them to stews, salads, or pasta dishes. Avocado is also rich in unsaturated fats. You can eat it as-is or use it in a smoothie or salad. Nuts and seeds such as almonds, walnuts, hazelnuts, cashews, pine nuts, sesame seeds, and pumpkin seeds are good sources of healthy fats. Avoid saturated fats found in cream, butter, lard, and red meat, as well as trans fats that are found in margarine or hydrogenated oils.

❖ **An occasional glass of red wine:** When taken in moderation, red wine may improve your heart's health by boosting good cholesterol levels (HDL), which can be attributed to special antioxidants found in red wine. It's all about moderation. Though no food is strictly off-limits, it's important to watch what you are eating, as well as your portion sizes, especially when eating foods containing high levels of saturated fat and high-calorie foods. Try as much as possible to eat natural and wholesome food for improved health.

❖ **Take time to be physically active and enjoy life:** The Mediterranean lifestyle is more relaxed compared to the typical western lifestyle, in the Mediterranean regions people take their time to enjoy meals with friends and family. Most walk or ride a bike to work instead of driving, and they take more vacations, thereby reducing stress.

How To Begin The Mediterranean Diet

The Mediterranean diet is an excellent strategy for eating healthier. These are the fundamentals:

- **Fresh fruits and vegetables:** Fresh fruits and vegetables of many different colors should take up most of the space on your platters. Salads and soups with legumes are common dishes in the Mediterranean region. Beans, peas, lentils, and split peas are just few of the legumes that fall under this umbrella.
- **Oils from Healthy Plants:** Extra-virgin olive oil, like other healthful plant oils, is a staple of the Mediterranean diet. You may prevent gastrointestinal distress from eating Mediterranean cuisine by gradually increasing your oil intake. Olive oil is excellent whether used as a dressing for salads or as a spread over whole-grain bread. Roasting vegetables after liberally coating them in olive oil yields delicious results, especially when applied to root vegetables but also to potatoes and eggplants. You may substitute seeds and nuts for processed and red meat in your diet, or eat them as a healthy snack on their own.
- **Unrefined Cereals and Whole Grains:** Make them a regular part of your diet. (When buying packaged bread products, be sure they don't have a harmful amount of salt by reading the nutrition labels.) You may also get whole wheat pasta and rice at supermarkets.

- **Dairy Products:** Consume yogurt and cheese in moderate amounts, but limit their use to condiments and garnishes. Dairy goods. Leafy salads and cold grain dishes, like tabbouleh (a bulgur wheat salad), benefit greatly from the addition of grated cheese or crumbled feta.
- **Fish:** Protein-rich foods like fish should make up the bulk of your diet, but you can also obtain some from other sources like chicken and eggs (three to four times per week).
- **Red Meat:** In order to maintain a healthy diet, you only need to eat one or two servings of raw, unprocessed red meat every week. Plan for Mediterranean Diet. Avoid "low fat" deli meats and other processed meats since they often include high levels of salt and other preservatives.
- **Alcoholic drinks and sodas of yesteryear:** In non-Muslim cultures that follow a diet similar to the Mediterranean diet, alcohol is often drunk in moderate amounts with meals. Each day, males should have no more than two drinks, while women should have no more than one.
- **Sweeteners:** The unhealthy refined carbs and trans fats found in large portions of sugary drinks, baked products, and rich desserts should be avoided. Cut down on white bread, white rice, and potatoes as well as sugary breakfast cereals and energy bars that are high in refined carbs. Rapid digestion of these carbs results in large increases in blood sugar and insulin. Similar spikes in blood sugar and insulin are seen after ingestion of complex carbohydrates as well.

How To Plan Your Mediterranean Diet

- **Base every meal around:**
  Vegetables and fruits (the darker in color, the more antioxidants they contain)
  Lentils, walnuts, and other nuts (like legumes and beans) Whole grains
  Olive oil as the main fat source (sub in margarine and butter)
- **Eat at least 2x/week:**
  Fish, seafood

Eat moderate portions five days a week or less:

Eggs, Cheese, and Poultry
Red wine (usual accompaniment to food).
Feminine: 1 glass each day; masculine: 2 glasses per day
- **Consume less often than other foods:**
  Red meat
  Fat-Saturated Sweets

The Rules

1. **Fruits, vegetables, cereals (mainly whole), olive oil, beans, nuts, legumes, seeds, herbs, and spices:** are all important components of a healthy diet. The Mediterranean diet is made up of all of these different components that make up the base of the pyramid. You should be sure to consume one of them at each of your meals.
2. **Fish and other marine foods:** These are essential components of the M. D., and you should try to eat them at least twice each week.

3.
4. **Eggs, yogurt, cheese, and chicken:** The average person in the M.D. consume a lower proportion of these substances (daily to weekly, depending on the food).

5. **Snacks, red meat, and sweets:** With the Mediterranean diet, red meat and sugary foods are eaten fewer times per week and in smaller amounts than in other diets. While this does not mean that you should never consume red meat again, you should try to limit how frequently you do so.

Mediterranean Shopping Guide

You should always choose the least processed foods, with a higher priority being on fresh and organic produce. It's advisable to shop around the grocery store's perimeter: This is usually where whole foods are found.

Here is a simple list you can use the next time you go food shopping:

FRUITS: grapes, apples, berries, citrus fruits, avocado, bananas, papaya, pineapple, etc.

VEGETABLES: broccoli, mushrooms, celery, carrots, kale, onions, leeks, eggplant, etc.

FROZEN VEGETABLES: healthy mixed veggie options

LEGUMES: beans, lentils, peas, etc.

GRAINS: all whole grains, including wholegrain pasta and wholegrain bread

NUTS: almonds, walnuts, cashews, hazelnuts, pistachios, pine nuts, etc.

SEEDS: pumpkin, hemp, sesame, sunflower, etc.

FISH: salmon, tuna, herring, sardines, sea bass, etc.

1. Shellfish varieties and shrimp

FREE-RANGE CHICKEN

BABY POTATOES AND SWEET POTATOES

CHEESE

NATURAL GREEK YOGURT

OLIVES

PASTURED EGGS

MEAT: goat, pork, and pastured beef

EXTRA VIRGIN OLIVE OIL

Eliminate all unhealthy foods not supported by the Mediterranean Diet from your kitchen, including candy, refined grain products, sodas, and artificially sweetened beverages, crackers, and other processed foods. If the only food you have in your home is healthy, that is what you are going to eat.

The Mediterranean Diet: What Can *You Eat*?

- ❖ **OLIVE OIL:** Per tablespoon serving: 120 calories, 0 g protein, 13 g fat (2 g saturated, 10 g monounsaturated), 0 g carbs, 0 fiber, and 0 sugars.
  Advantages: Some research suggests that switching from animal-based saturated fats like butter to plant-based monounsaturated fats like olive oil may reduce the risk of cardiovascular disease by as much as 19 percent.
- ❖ **TOMATO:** Serving of 1 cup, contains 32 Cal., 1.5g protein, 0g fat, 7g carbs, 2g fiber, 5g sugar.

Advantages: high concentrations of the potent antioxidant lycopene have been linked to a decreased risk of developing some cancers, including prostate and breast cancers. To further protect against cardiovascular disease, tomatoes may also include compounds that prevent blood clots. This might be possible since tomatoes have been shown to reduce the risk of blood clots.

❖ **FATTY FISH (SALMON):** 1 Small Fillet contains 272 Cal., 44g protein, 9g fat, 0g carbs, 0g fiber.
  Advantages: Fatty fish may be an excellent source of omega-3 fatty acids whose frequent ingestion is recommended. Two servings of fish each week, especially fatty fish like salmon, may be beneficial to cardiovascular health, according to some research.

❖ **WALNUTS:** You may get 14 hazelnut halves for $1, or $1 for every ounce. Included are 185 calories, 4 g of protein, 3 g of saturated fat, 3 g of monounsaturated fat, and 13 g of polyunsaturated fat, 4 g of carbohydrates, 2 g of fiber, and 1 gram of sugar.
  Advantages: In addition to lowering your LDL cholesterol, these nuts may improve your gut bacteria (and hence your digestive health) and include heart-healthy polyunsaturated fats.

❖ **Chickpeas:** ½ Cup Serving 160 Cal., 10g protein, 2g fat, 26g carbohydrate, 5g fiber
  Advantages: The main ingredient in hummus, has a high fiber level, which is beneficial for digestive health. nutrients including iron, zinc, folic acid, and magnesium, which all have benefits for fat loss.

❖ **ARUGULA:** Five calories, half a gram of protein, zero g of fat, one gram of carbohydrates, one gram of fiber, and zero g of sugar may be found in a single cup of arugula.
  Advantages: Consuming enough dark, leafy greens like arugula is essential to this diet because of the many health advantages they provide. If you eat leafy greens often (more than six times a week), you may reduce your risk of developing Alzheimer's disease. The Mediterranean diet is famous for its emphasis on eating several leafy greens throughout the week.

❖ **POMEGRANATE:** Nutritional Information has 72 calories, 1.5 g of protein, 1 gram of fat, 16 g of carbs, 4 g of fiber, and 12 g of sugar per half-cup serving.
  Advantages: The bright red pigment of this fruit comes from the high polyphenol content, which has anti-inflammatory and antioxidant qualities. It's also been hypothesized that pomegranates help stop cancer cells from multiplying.

❖ **LENTILS:** A half-cup serving has 115 calories, 9 g of protein, 0 g of fat, 20 g of carbohydrates, 8 g of fiber, and 2 g of sugar.
  Advantages: include a 20% reduction in blood sugar levels when replacing half of your meal of a high-glycemic carbohydrate (like rice) with lentils.

❖ **FARRO:** One-fourth of a cup of raw FARRO has 200 calories and 7 g of protein. Sugars 0g, fiber 7g, carbohydrates 37g, fat 1.5g.
  Advantages: This eating plan includes whole grains like farro that are high in fiber and other nutrients. The satiating fiber and protein in this grain make it an excellent choice. Consumption of whole grains is associated with a reduced risk of several diseases.

❖ **YOGURT TYPE GREEK:** Totaling 147 calories, 20 g of protein, 4 g of fat (2 g of saturated fat, 1 gram of monounsaturated fat, and 0 g of polyunsaturated fat), 8 g of carbs, 0 g of fiber, and 7 g of sugars can be found in a single serving of GRK Yogurt.
  Advantages: The foods below are rich in calcium even if dairy is not consumed in large amounts. By switching to low- or no-fat options, you may be able to reduce the amount of saturated fat you eat.

If You're Following The Mediterranean Diet, What Shouldn't You Eat?

A great deal of food undergoes some kind of processing. The canning process requires the beans to be treated, sometimes known as cooked, before they can be packaged. When olives are squeezed to get olive oil, the oil has been refined. Yet, when we talk about cutting down on processed foods, we advocate avoiding items like frozen dinners because of the excessive amount of salt that they contain. In the same vein, soda, sweets, and desserts should only be drunk in small amounts.

- ❖ **Red Meat, Prepared with Prose:** With a Mediterranean diet, you should try to reduce your consumption of red meat like steak. What about red meats that have been processed, like hot dogs and bacon? It is recommended that you steer clear of or limit your consumption of these items as much as you can.

- ❖ **Butter:** In addition to olive oil, the Mediterranean diet is the only one that should not include butter. Instead of butter, you should use olive oil since it is healthier for your heart and contains less saturated fat than butter does. In comparison, one tablespoon of butter has seven g of saturated fat, whereas one tablespoon of olive oil only contains around two g.

- ❖ **Refined Cereals and Grains:** The Mediterranean diet focuses heavily on the consumption of whole grains. Foods such as farro, millet, couscous, and brown rice are included in this category. When you are on this diet, you have to cut down on your intake of refined carbohydrates like white bread and pasta as much as you can.

- ❖ **Wine and Alcohol:** If you are attempting to adhere to the principles of the Mediterranean diet, one of the things that is highly suggested is drinking a glass of red wine before supper. This is due to the fact that drinking red wine has been associated with several health advantages, most notably for the cardiovascular system. It is recommended that women and men over the age of 65 have no more than one drink of alcohol per day, while males under the age of 65 should have no more than two drinks of alcohol per day. One drink is often considered to equal 5 ounces of wine, 12 ounces of beer, or 1.5 ounces of 80-proof liquor. These are the conventional measurements.

Purchasing, Using, And Storing Olive Oil And Its Critical Importance

Olive oil, similar to butter and coconut oil, is considered to be a "superfood" due to the fact that even a little quantity has a disproportionately high concentration of nutrients. If you include the oil into your typical cooking routine and eat at least a little bit of it on a daily basis, your body may be able to enjoy the advantages of the oil over the course of time.

- ❖ **ACID OLEIC:** Oleic acid, a kind of long-chain fatty acid, makes almost 75% of olive oil. Even just one teaspoon a day of this omega-9 supplement may make a difference in the battle against aggressive breast cancer (but researchers still recommend obtaining oleic acid from other whole foods like nuts, seeds, and avocados). Also, oleic acid strengthens the cell membranes of our blood vessels, which enables our blood vessels to better handle the pressure of the regular flow of blood and the other everyday processes of the body.

- ❖ **VITAMIN TYPE E:** Vitamin E is an antioxidant that helps protect cells from harm caused by free radicals and also helps repair damage that has already been done. Vitamin E is essential to the maintenance of healthy cells throughout our bodies. It promotes the speedy recovery of the skin and naturally thins the blood, which prevents improper clumping of the platelets in the bloodstream.

- ❖ **POLYPHENOLS:** Olive oil contains at least 18 distinct types of phenolic compounds, several of which are among the most powerful antioxidants found in nature. Some of them limit the oxidation of LDL cholesterol in the blood arteries, which prevents it from possibly becoming calcified. Another kind prevents the growth of disease-causing bacteria in the digestive system, hence reducing the risk of gastrointestinal conditions including ulcers. The long-term effects of these polyphenols include improved cognitive function, decreased risk of developing type 2 diabetes, and protection against cardiovascular disease and neurological illnesses.

- ❖ **OLEOCANTHAL:** Oleocanthal is a kind of polyphenol that is known for its ability to reduce inflammation (essentially blocking two enzymes). Olive oils with stronger flavors have a higher concentration of oleocanthal, and the anti-inflammatory effects of 3 and a half tablespoons of olive oil are about comparable to those of a 200-milligram pill of ibuprofen. An exceptional way to naturally manage the pain and swelling associated with arthritis.

Purchasing Olive Oil: Suggestions

- Extra-virgin olive oil that has been "cold-pressed". Olives, when subjected to the appropriate amount of pressure, may have these oils extracted from them, and are not necessary use of other methods.
- The taste of extra-virgin olive oil, which is obtained from the fruit during the first stages of processing, is regarded by most people as having the purest and most genuine representation of olive oil's natural flavor.
- Olives are typically pressed twice before producing virgin olive oil. In spite of the fact that it will be squeezed out using pressure, it will taste noticeably more sour than when it was first produced. It may be beneficial to test out both choices and decide which one best suits your needs and preferences if the price difference between them is significant.
- Olive oil that has been filtered and packaged in a container with the label "light" has had part of the fruit pulp and peel removed. This is a comment about color, and it has nothing to do with the amount of calories or fat in the food. Because the filtering process may remove some of the health advantages of olive oil.
- Since it gives a totally inaccurate impression of the contents of the bottle, you shouldn't purchase one bottle that's branded "pure" oil. This olive oil is a blend of refined extra virgin olive oil, virgin olive oil, and olive oils that aren't of very good quality overall. Olive oil is often the only thing that is written on the label of these bottles. The olive harvest takes place in the autumn, and the oil that is produced from those olives is made accessible the following year. On the bottle of olive oil, there needs to be a prominently displayed harvest date. If you go about it in this manner, you won't need to be concerned about acquiring oil that has gone rancid and old. Also, you may make an estimate about how much longer you will be able to make use of it.

The Olive Oil Vault

The proper storage of olive oil is essential since its shelf life is much shorter than that of other types of lipids. It's likely that if you store your pricey olive oil in an unsuitable manner, you might speed up the oil's degradation. Oil that has been tainted with rancidity has a detrimental effect, not only on the taste of the oil but also on its structural integrity.

- Dark and opaque (but yet see-through) glass must be used for the bottle. If you want to preserve the quality of your oil for as long as possible, you should avoid using transparent glass.
- While the bottle is not being used, be sure to keep the cap on it. Not only does light contribute to the decomposition of oil, but also air does.
- It is important to store the oil at a temperature that is on the lower end of the scale, between 57- and 70-degrees Fahrenheit. If your kitchen is often warmer than this, you may want to think about relocating to a closet, basement, or garage where the temperature is naturally lower.
- It is not a good idea to keep your cooking oil in a stylish container made of transparent glass and fitted with a pour spout and keep it near your stove. This goes against every single regulation that pertains to the correct way to store olive oil. Stay away from that area.

The Significance Of Omega-3

Omega-3 fatty acids are essential nutrients, so be sure to get enough of them in your diet. Since your body doesn't make them, you have to receive them from what you consume. Omega-3 fatty acids (EPA) come in a few different forms, but the three most important ones are docosahexaenoic acid (DHA), eicosapentaenoic acid (EPA), and alpha-linolenic acid (ALA).

ALA is most often found in plant meals, whereas DHA and EPA are typically found in animal foods and algae. Many foods, including walnuts, fatty fish, fish oils, flax seeds, chia seeds, and flaxseed oil, are rich in omega-3 fatty acids. The same is true with chia seeds and flax seeds.

1. MAY SUPPORT HEART HEALTH

Here attacks are the leading cause of death in the United States.

Cholesterol levels: According to research, it increases the amount of "good" HDL cholesterol in the body. Nevertheless, it did not seem to lower levels of LDL cholesterol, also known as "bad" cholesterol.

Triglyceride levels: may be reduced by 15-30%.

Blood Reveal: Tiny doses may help those with high blood pressure feel better.

Plaque: It may reduce the risk of arterial plaque developing in patients and may also make existing arterial plaque more stable and secure.

Fatal Arrhythmias: It's possible that those at risk for fatal arrhythmias may have fewer fatal arrhythmias as a consequence. Arrhythmias, or abnormal heart rhythms, have been linked to an increased risk of heart attack in certain people.

2. HELP TREAT CERTAIN MENTAL DISORDERS

About 60% of your brain is made up of fat, and a large amount of that is omega- 3fatty acids. Therefore, omega- 3 fatty acids are crucial for normal brain function; low levels of these fats in the blood have been linked to mental health issues.

3. MAY AID WEIGHT LOSS

A body mass index (BMI) of 30 or above, or a waist circumference more than 85 centimeters, is considered to be clinically obese. Worldwide, it is estimated that 39% of individuals are overweight and another 13% are clinically obese. There has been a concerning and frightening increase in the prevalence of obesity. Supplementing with omega-3 fatty acids may improve body composition and cardiovascular disease risk factors in obese people.

4. MAY SUPPORT EYE HEALTH

Omega 3 - fats are essential for the proper functioning of both the brain and the eyes. Inadequate intake of omega-3 fatty acids has been linked to an increased risk of developing eye issues..

5. MAY REDUCE INFLAMMATION

When under assault, the immune system triggers inflammation to repair damaged tissue and fight off infection. However, inflammation is linked to serious conditions including diabetes, heart disease, and dementia. Omega-3 fatty acids, which have been shown to reduce inflammation, might be useful in treating this condition.

6. MAY SUPPORT HEALTHY SKIN

Omega-3 fatty acids are abundant in the skin, the body's largest organ. Spending too much time in the sun, together with the natural aging process, may take a toll on your skin's health.

7. MAY SUPPORT PREGNANCY AND EARLY LIFE

While pregnant and breastfeeding, moms should consume enough omega-3 fatty acids to give their infants with the nutrients necessary for healthy growth and development. Pregnant or breastfeeding mothers who take fish oil supplements may see improvements in their children's motor skills. However, if this enhances learning or IQ, remains unclear. Prenatal supplementation has been demonstrated to improve infants' visual acuity and decrease their risk of developing allergies as children.

Foods Rich in Omega-3

- Eat nothing that isn't completely natural, fresh, or entire.
- Consume between five and ten servings of fruits and vegetables on a daily basis, and increase the amount of legumes, and seeds you consume.
- To boost the amount of omega-3 fatty acids in your diet, increase the amount of fish, walnuts, flaxseed oil, and green leafy vegetables you consume. It is possible that eating the necessary quantity of omega-3 fats in your diet may be accomplished by consuming either one gram of an omega-3 fatty acid supplement or two servings of salted almonds per week.
- Consume beverages such as water, tea, low-fat diary, and red wine (two drinks daily for men, one drink daily for women).

- Eat learn forms of protein such as skinless chicken, fish, and lean cuts of red meat in your diet.
- Reduce your intake of saturated fats and avoid foods that contain trans fats as much as possible. This includes avoiding meals that are frozen, hard margarine, professionally baked items, the majority of packaged and processed snack foods, and high-fat dairy products. It also means avoiding margarine that is solid at room temperature, processed meat such as bacon, sausage, and deli meats, among other examples
- No more satiety-inducing banquets. Both sugar and white flour contribute to an increase in blood sugar levels, which in turn stimulates the pancreas to produce insulin. Glycemic meals are rich in both sugar and white flour. Insulin levels that are persistently raised are linked to both weight gain and the development of atherosclerosis in the arteries.

How to Lose Weight With The Mediterranean Diet

- Plant-based food, such as vegetables, fruits, whole grains, legumes, nuts, and seeds, as well as prepared meals like pasta and extra-virgin olive oil, constitute the basis of the Mediterranean diet. According to the consensus of medical professionals, this is the healthiest way to eat. It's possible that following a Mediterranean diet can help you lose weight, but that wasn't the intention behind the diet in the first place. Dieting as a means of achieving and maintaining a healthy weight loss goal may be a viable and tenable strategy. Here are some of the reasons why you may want to think about adopting a Mediterranean diet if your goal is to reduce your body fat percentage. The only thing you need to do to get started is to be organized and make a plan for the food you will be serving. Here are a few of the most important points:
- **Choose between two breakfasts:** The majority of individuals adhere to a certain pattern for breakfast, therefore the only variable that may shift is the food that is consumed at breakfast. Oatmeal, Greek yogurt, and eggs are all potential choices for breakfast while following a Mediterranean diet. For breakfast, you ought to satiate yourself with fruits, veggies, or any mix of the two.
- **Make a schedule for two or three easy meals every day:** When you limit the options available to you, the number of different meals that can be prepared with a given amount of goods will decrease. You will spend less time in the kitchen by following this technique, your dinners will be more interesting as a result, and you will have leftovers to munch on later. Your menu has the potential to be interesting and engaging if you are given the opportunity to choose new dishes to make every week.
- **Keep simple foods:** If you are less skilled in the kitchen, it is recommended that you choose products that require little efforts, such as salad greens, frozen vegetables, eggs, canned tuna, and canned or boxed pulses (such as chickpeas and lentils that have been soaked). If you are less skilled in the kitchen, it is recommended that you choose products that require little efforts, such as salad greens, frozen vegetables, eggs, canned tuna, and canned or boxed pulses (such as chickpeas and lentils that have been soaked). Quinoa, brown rice, and oats are all examples of straightforward whole-grain selections.
- **Prepare your snacks in advance:** Whether you are preparing snacks in preparation or making them on the go, you should switch from packaged snacks to snacks made from whole foods. There are a few fast choices available, such as eating a piece of fruit with almonds, slicing veggies and eating them with hummus, or eating olive tapenade.
- **Put more of an emphasis on how enjoyable eating can be:** There is no such thing as a restricted diet in the Mediterranean region. Instead, appreciation is shown toward the culinary arts, and mealtimes are organized with the goal of maximizing pleasure. This component of creating a good connection with food and developing sustainable eating habits is sometimes neglected in weight reduction strategies, despite the fact that it is essential to both goals.

BREAKFAST

1. Almond Mascarpone Dumplings

Readiness Time: 5-7 minutes Time needed to cook: 5-10 minutes Quantity of Meals: 6

Required Material:

- Granular wheat flour: 1 cup
- Flour, general use, unbleached: one cup
- Almond flour: 1/4 mug
- Egg use only whites: 4
- Mascarpone cheese: three ounces
- EVO oil: one tsp
- Apple juice: two tsp
- Butter: 1 tbsp
- Honey: 1-quarter cup

Step-By-Step Procedure:

1. Sift the two flours together in a large basin. Throw in some almonds and mix well. In a second dish, whip together the egg whites, cheese, oil, and juice using an electric mixer.
2. Use a dough hook or your hands to combine the flour and egg white on medium speed to form a dough forms.
3. Get one liter of water boiling in a stockpot of suitable size. Put some dough into the boiling water by pushing it in with a spoon.
4. Continue cooking until all the dumplings have floated to the surface (5-10 minutes). You may cook a lot of dumplings at once without worrying about crowding the pan. Drain on paper towels after being removed using a slotted spoon.
5. Warm up a sauté pan of the right size. Loose the butter until it has golden brown color, then add the dumplings to the pan. Honey should be served on plates and spread out.

Dietary Composition: Caloric Intake: 500, Quantity of fat: 25g, Quantity of Protein: 10g, Quantity of Carbohydrates: 30g, Quantity of Fiber: 2g, Quantity of Cholesterol: 200mg, Quantity of Sodium: 200mg

2. Avocado Toast

Readiness Time: 4-5 minutes Time needed to cook: 2 minutes Quantity of Meals: 4

Required Material:

- Ripe avocados that are peeled: 2
- Freshly squeezed lemon juice: to taste
- Finely cut Mint: 2 tbsp, with extra for the garnish
- Salt and pepper, should be used to taste
- Huge rye bread cut: Four big slices
- Crumbled feta cheese: 80 g

Step-By-Step Procedure:

1. Use a fork to coarsely crush the avocados in a medium bowl, then incorporate in the lemon juice and mint.
2. Spice to taste using salt and pepper at your disposal.
3. Toast the bread on a grill or in the oven until golden brown, then spread each slice

with a quarter of the avocado mixture and cheese. Decorate with more mint and eat.

Dietary Composition: Caloric Intake 350, Quantity of fat: 25 g, Quantity of Protein: 6 g, Quantity of Carbohydrates: 30 g, Quantity of Fiber: 12 g, Quantity of Cholesterol: 0-80mg (depending on additional toppings), Quantity of Sodium: 300mg

3. Breakfast Burrito

Readiness Time: 15-17 minutes Time needed to cook: 5 minutes Quantity of Meals: 6

Required Material:

- Tortillas, whole 10-inch: Six
- Whole eggs: 9
- Baby spinach, already cleaned and dried: 2 mugs
- Black olives (sliced) and Tomatoes (Raw Diced): three tablespoons each
- Optional Salsa.
- Feta cheese, crumbled: Half cup
- Refried beans canned: 3-quarter cup

Step-By-Step Procedure:

1. Fill a shallow pan with nonstick cooking spray. It takes around 5 minutes to scramble eggs and tomatoes until the eggs are solid.
2. Dry the mixture out by stirring in spinach, black olives, and sun-dried tomatoes. Cover the dish after include the feta cheese inside until it melts.
3. Fill each tortilla with two tbsp of refried beans, then divide the egg mixture equally between the tortillas and the burritos.
4. Grill the burritos over the direct flame on a comal or in a frying pan until they are gently browned.
5. Top with salsa and fruit (if desired) and serve hot. Before wrapping it for freezing, make sure it has cooled completely.
6. If reheating, microwave for twenty seconds (in parchment paper) and serve immediately.

Dietary Composition: Caloric Intake 600, Quantity of fat: 40 g, Quantity of Protein: 30 g, Quantity of Carbohydrates: 60 g, Quantity of Fiber: 3 g, Quantity of Cholesterol: 400mg, Quantity of Sodium: 1g

4. Breakfast Couscous

Readiness Time: 18 minutes Time needed to cook: 18 minutes Quantity of Meals: 4

Required Material:

- Cinnamon stick (about 2 inches in length): 1
- milk, 1% fat: Three mugs
- Couscous, type whole wheat uncooked: 1 cup
- Unrefined Brown Sugar: Six Teaspoons
- Dried currants: 1-quarter cup
- Apricots, dried and already chopped: 1/2 cup
- Sea salt: 1/4 tsp
- Butter: Four tbsp

Step-By-Step Procedure:

1. Sauté the milk and cinnamon for three minutes over medium heat, stirring occasionally, but avoiding a boil.
2. Incorporate the couscous, 4 teaspoons of sugar, the currants, the apricots, and the salt into a bowl and set the pan aside. Leave the mixture to settle for at least 15 minutes with the lid on the bowl.
3. Take out the cinnamon stick and serve the soup in four dishes, topping each with sugar and a dollop of melted butter.
4. Quickly serve

Dietary Composition: Caloric Intake 200, Quantity of Carbohydrates: 40 g, Quantity of Protein: 5g, Quantity of fat: 4g, Quantity of Fiber: 4g

5. Breakfast Stir Fry

Readiness Time: 5 minutes Time needed to cook: 8 minutes Quantity of Meals: 4

Required Material:

- Evo oil: Only 1 Tbsp
- Green peppers and onions: 4 (two of each)
- Tomatoes (chopped): Four
- Salt: half a teaspoon
- Egg: one

Step-By-Step Procedure:

1. Warm the EVO oil; once hot, put the green pepper in, cook for 2 mins, stirring regularly.
2. Three more minutes of cooking time should be allotted with the lid on.
3. Stirring periodically, cook the onion for 2 minutes.
4. When the tomatoes are soft and the sauce has a thick, season and simmer the mixture uncovered for a few more minutes.
5. After beating the egg, sprinkle it over the tomato mixture (without stirring) and heat for 1 minute.
6. Garnishes may include cucumbers, feta cheese, and black olives.

Dietary Composition: Caloric Intake 500, Quantity of fat: 25g, Quantity of Protein: 25g, Quantity of Carbohydrates: 50 g, Quantity of Fiber: 4g, Quantity of Cholesterol: 400mg, Quantity of Sodium: 500mg

6. Breakfast Wrap

Readiness Time: 10-13 minutes Time needed to cook: 10 minutes Quantity of Meals: 2

Required Material:

- Spinach, harvested fresh peak: Half cups
- Egg whites, 4
- Sun-dried tomatoes (type Bella), Wraps (type mixed-grain): 2 of each
- Crumbled feta, 1/2 cup

Step-By-Step Procedure:

1. For approximately 4 minutes, fry the greens (spinach), egg whites, and tomatoes.
2. Flip it over and continue cooking for another 4 minutes.
3. Wraps may be heated for 15 seconds in the microwave before being filled with the egg mixture, sprinkled with crumbled feta cheese, and rolled up.
4. Before serving, cut each wrap in half lengthwise.

Dietary Composition: Caloric Intake 301, Quantity of Protein: 15g, Quantity of fat: 18g, Carbs: 19g, Quantity of Fiber: 3g

7. Cheese Pies in Yogurt Pastry

Readiness Time: 16 minutes Time needed to cook: 35 minutes Quantity of Meals: 10

Required Material:

- Large Eggs: Two
- EVO oil: 1/2 mug
- Unsweetened yogurt: 3/4 mug
- Salt: 1 tsp.
- Sifted self-rising flour: three and a half cups.
- Feta cheese, ricotta: Two cups (One of each)
- Shredded Gruyère or Graviera: 1/4 cup
- Egg Yolk: One Large;
- Nutmeg: just half tsp
- Pepper: 1-quarter tsp;
- Cream and Mint: One Tablespoon (each)
- Finely Chopped Sesame seeds: half cup

Step-By-Step Procedure:

1. Whip together one egg, oil, and yogurt. Combine now salt and flour and with a wooden spoon or your hands amalgamate well.
2. Pass the dough to a flat top and knead it for a few minutes, or until the flour is

completely absorbed. The dough should be pliable, somewhat sticky, and easy to work with. Don't touch the dough for now; just wrap it in plastic.

3. A temperature of 350 degrees Fahrenheit should be set on the oven. In a large dish, mix the one egg remaining with the 2 cheeses, nutmeg, pepper, and mint. Mix everything together using a wooden spoon.

4. Make 20 equal-sized balls, about the dimension of an egg. Press a sphere of dough into a disc approximately three inches thick using the palm of your hand. Put the quantity of full teaspoon of the cheese compound in the dough's middle.

5. Make a crescent shape by folding over half of the dough over the filling. Pinching the dough ends together will keep the cheese inside.

6. Lay it on a baking sheet covered with parchment foil and repeat the steps with the rest of the dough.

7. Whip now egg yolk and cream, when are completely combined, spread the mixture on top of each pie. Top with sesame seeds.

8. Put the pies inside the oven on the middle rack and make cook for 30 mins.

9. Warm them up or keep them at a comfortable temperature. Refrigerated pies have a five-day shelf life if sealed tightly.

Dietary Composition: Caloric Intake 330, Quantity of Protein: 13g, Quantity of fat: 23g, Carbs: 18g, Quantity of Fiber: 2g

8. Egg and Sausage Breakfast Casserole

Readiness Time: 2 hours' Time needed to cook: 1 hour and 15 minutes Quantity of Meals: 12

Required Material:

For the crust:

- Russet potatoes, they grow peeled and sliced: Two pounds
- Olive oil: three tablespoons

- Pepper in powder and salt: each 3/4 tsp.

The casserole:

- Turkey sausage: 12 ounces, chopped
- Big eggs: 6
- Only white eggs: 4
- Shredded cheddar: A total of 3/4 cups
- Green onions: Four
- Sweet peppers, diced: 1-quarter cup
- Cottage cheese, low-fat: 16 oz.
- Milk, Skim: 1/3 mug

Step-By-Step Procedure:

1. Warm your oven to 425°F. Proceed after buttering a 9-by-13-inch pan. Towel-dry the potato.

2. Toss the potatoes in a medium bowl with the remaining olive oil, salt, and pepper until evenly coated.

3. Spread the ingredients evenly over the bottom and up the sides of a greased baking dish and bake for 20 minutes until golden brown.

For casserole:

4. Reduce the heat in the oven to 375 degrees F.

5. Turkey sausage is virtually done after 2 minutes in a large pan.

6. Cook onions and sweet pepper for two more minutes. Mix cheese, milk, eggs, and egg whites.

7. Bake for 50 minutes after mixing in the turkey sausage and pouring the mixture over a potato crust. Serve cold and in 12 individual portions. Enjoy!

Dietary Composition: Caloric Intake 500, Quantity of fat: 35g, Quantity of Protein: 30g, Quantity of Carbohydrates: 20g, Quantity of Fiber: 2g, Quantity of Cholesterol: 600mg, Quantity of Sodium: 1g

9. <u>Energizing Breakfast Protein Bars</u>

Readiness Time: 10-13 minutes Time needed to cook: 5 minutes Quantity of Meals: 6

Required Material:

- Pistachios: two tablespoons
- Flaxseeds, Natural Peanut Butter, Pecan: a 1-quarter cup of each
- Flakes of Spelt: 1 1/4 mug
- Oil: Two tbsp
- Honey and: Half cup
- Salt: A Pinch
- Dried Cherries: 1/2 mug
- Vanilla extract: 1/2 teaspoons

Step-By-Step Procedure:

1. Then, get an oven ready at 325F and oil the baking sheet gently.
2. Prepare a tin with foil paper and oil. In a dish, combine fruits, pecans, pistachios, spelt, flaxseed, salt.
3. Honey, oil, peanut butter, and vanilla extract should be melted together over low to medium heat, with the ingredients regularly stirred.
4. Combine this liquid with the dry components. After putting the batter into the prepared baking dish, level it out.
5. Bake: when the top is golden and the edges start to separate from the pan is ready.
6. Once has been done, remove it from the tin and cut it into smaller pieces on a cutting board.
7. Once chilled, place in an airtight container lined with parchment paper. The bars may be stored for up to a week after opening. Enjoy!

Dietary Composition: Caloric Intake 250, Quantity of Protein: 20g, Quantity of Carbohydrates: 30g, Quantity of fat: 12g, Quantity of Fiber: 5g

10. <u>Feta & Quinoa Egg Muffins</u>

Readiness Time: 14 minutes Time needed to cook: 30 minutes Quantity of Meals: 12

Required Material:

- Frozen spinach: Two cups
- Cherry Tomato, already sliced and chopped: One mug
- Onion: 1/2 mug
- 8 eggs
- Quinoa, already cooked: 1 cup
- Kalamata olives: 1/2 cup
- Fresh oregano: One tablespoon
- Sunflower oil with a high oleic content, + more for greasing muffin cups: at least 2 tsp
- Feta cheese: One cup
- Salt: 1-quarter teaspoon

Step-By-Step Procedure:

1. Prepare a 12-cup muffin tray or use silicone muffin cups (both should be oiled) and insert them in the oven at 350 degrees Fahrenheit.
2. Gather your ingredients and heat a pan to medium. The next step is to add some onion and vegetable oil and cook it down for two minutes. Toss in tomato and cook for one min, then add the spinach and cook for another min, or until wilted. Take off the heat and stir in the olives and oregano.
3. Blend or whisk the eggs together in a blender or large mixing dish. Add eggs, quinoa, feta, vegetable combination, and salt to a mixing bowl (or a blender). Mix well by stirring.
4. Muffins should be baked in a pre-heated oven (30 mins). Distribute the batter equally among muffin pans.
5. Cooling for 5 mins before serving or save for tomorrow and reheat in the microwave.

Dietary Composition: Caloric Intake 200, Quantity of Protein: 12g, Quantity of Carbohydrates: 20g, Quantity of fat: 12g, Quantity of Fiber: 3g

11. Fruit-Stuffed French Toast

Readiness Time: 12 minutes Time needed to cook: 20 minutes Quantity of Meals: 6

Required Material:

- Olive oil: Half tsp
- Loaves challah bread: 3 small or medium
- Fresh fruit seasonal: 1 pint
- Egg: 2 (whole) and 4 only whites
- Dairy products (skim milk and nonfat plain yogurt): the same quantity of 1/4 cup each
- Sugar:1-quarter cup
- Orange, only juice: One mug

Step-By-Step Procedure:

1. The oven has to be preheated to 375 degrees F. Prepare a pan for baking and spray it with oil.
2. Bread should be trimmed into thick (2 1/2–3 inch) pieces.
   Cut the challah in half lengthwise to obtain three thick slices. Cut off the bottom crust to make a pocket.
3. To prepare the fruit for stuffing the bread, peel it if required and then dice it into big pieces. Fill bread pocket.
4. Whisk the egg whites and yolks together. Immerse the bread in the egg mixture and let it soak up the flavor. Get a baking sheet ready and lay out the bread. Ten minutes at 400 degrees, flipped, and another ten minutes at 400 degrees.
5. While the bread is in the oven, reduce the orange juice by half and thicken it into syrup in a small pot. Prepare your French toast by slicing it in half across the diagonal. Top with a little bit of yogurt, some fruit juice, and sugar, and serve.

Dietary Composition: Caloric Intake 450 calories, Quantity of fat: 20g, Quantity of Protein: 12g, Quantity of Carbohydrates: 50g, Quantity of Fiber: 2g, Quantity of Cholesterol: 150mg, Quantity of Sodium: 250mg

12. Fruity Nutty Muesli

Readiness Time: 1 hour and 6 minutes Time needed to cook: 10 minutes Quantity of Meals: 2

Required Material:

- Almonds, chopped: 1/3 cup
- Oats, already toasted: 3-quarter cup
- Milk: 1/2 cup
- Green apple: 1/2
- Honey: Two tbsp
- Greek yogurt: Half mug

Step-By-Step Procedure:

1. Before you do anything else, heat your oven to 375 degrees. Lay the almonds in a single layer on a tin, and bake for approximately 10 mins.
2. After the toasted oats have cooled, stir in the milk and yogurt and cover the bowl. After an hour in the fridge with this combination, the oats would soften.
3. Split the muesli in half and add the apple and honey to each bowl.

Dietary Composition: Caloric Intake: 329, Quantity of fat: 18.7g, Quantity of Carbohydrates:

35g, Quantity of Fiber: 4.8g, Quantity of Protein: 8.5g

13. Healthy Quinoa

Readiness Time: 12 minutes Time needed to cook: 20 minutes Quantity of Meals: 4

Required Material:

- Almonds: 1 mug
- Milk: 2 cups
- Sea salt: a pinch
- Honey: 2 tbsp.
- Cinnamon: 1 tsp.
- Quinoa: One cup
- Fruits dried (apricots and dates): 5 plus 2
- Vanilla extract: One tsp

Step-By-Step Procedure:

1. First toast the almonds (five mins), until they are golden brown.
2. Spiced quinoa should be heated with a pinch of cinnamon.
3. While stirring continually, add milk and salt in the saucepan with quinoa. Cover saucepan and cook for 15 mins after mixture has started to boil.
4. Soften honey, apricots, dates, and vanilla essence in a saucepan with half of the almonds.
5. Place in serving dishes and top with the remaining almonds.

Dietary Composition: Caloric Intake: 170, Quantity of Protein: 8g, Quantity of fat: 4 g, Quantity of Carbohydrates: 30g, Quantity of Fiber: 5g

14. Homemade Greek Yogurt

Readiness Time:16 hours and 15 minutes Time needed to cook: 15 minutes Quantity of Meals:16 cups

Required Material:

- Whole milk, 16 mugs

- A half cup of plain, full-fat, active-culture yogurt)

Step-By-Step Procedure:

1. Pre-heat the oven to at least 200 degrees Fahrenheit. The milk should be reaching to a boil in a pan. Lower over medium heat for 15 minutes, uncovered. Then put away from heat.
2. Using a candy thermometer, bring the temperature of the milk down to between 110- and 115 degrees Fahrenheit. In a dish, combine half cup warm milk and yogurt and stir until the mixture is lukewarm. After reintroducing the milk and yogurt to the saucepan, mix them well.
3. Put the oven's door shut. A low temperature in the oven makes plastic containers safe, so fill them with the milk and yogurt mixture and place them on tin. It takes 8-12 hours for yogurt to set (check at 8 hours).
4. For best results, refrigerate the yogurt for at least 4 hours but no more than 2 weeks.

Dietary Composition: Caloric Intake: 150, Quantity of Protein: 13g, Quantity of fat: 9g, Quantity of Carbohydrates: 6g, Quantity of Fiber: 0

15. Mediterranean Pancakes

Readiness Time: 7-10 minutes Time needed to cook: 25 minutes Quantity of Meals: 16 Pancakes

Required Material:

- Rolled oats, one cup;
- Flax seeds: Two tbsp.
- All-purpose flour: 1/2 cup
- Baking soda: one teaspoon
- Salt from the sea: 1/4 tsp
- EVO oil, raw honey: the same quantity of 2 tbsp
- Big eggs: 2
- Fat-free Greek yogurt: Two cups
- Toppings of fresh fruit, syrup, or both

Step-By-Step Procedure:

1. In a high-powered blender, combine the oats, flour, flax seeds, baking soda, and salt for 30 seconds.
2. Add in some eggs, yogurt, honey, and EVO oil, and blend until smooth. If you want a thicker combination, wait at least 20 minutes.
3. Brush some oil into pan and warm. Put the batter in the skillet a quarter cup at a time.
4. Cupcakes need 2 minutes in the oven to get a golden-brown puffy top.
5. Cook for a further two minutes on the opposite side, or until golden brown.
6. Pancakes may be kept warm in the oven if they are placed on a baking sheet immediately after baking.
7. Add seasonings to taste before serving.

Dietary Composition: Caloric Intake: 300, Quantity of Protein: 12g, Quantity of Carbohydrates: 40g, Quantity of fat: 15g, Quantity of Fiber: 3g

16. Mediterranean Veggie Omelet

Readiness Time: 10-13 minutes Time needed to cook: 15 minutes Quantity of Meals: 4

Required Material:

- EVO oil: One tbsp.
- Fennel bulb: Two cups
- Artichoke hearts, soaked in water, drained: 1-quarter cup
- Roma tomato: 1
- Eggs: 6
- Green olives: One-quarter mug
- Sea salt: ¼ tsp
- Cheese, type goat: ½ cup
- black pepper: ½ tsp
- parsley, dill, or basil: 2 tbsp.

Step-By-Step Procedure:
1. Put extra virgin olive oil in an ovenproof skillet and heat it until it's ready to use.
2. The fennel needs around 5 minutes in the pan to get soft. For three minutes, or until

softened, cook the artichoke hearts, olives, and tomatoes.
3. Crack eggs into a dish and season with salt & pepper. Two minutes into cooking time, stir the egg mixture into the veggies.
4. The omelet is done when the cheese on top has set and the oven has reached 350 degrees Fahrenheit.
5. To garnish, try using parsley, dill, or basil.
6. After transferring the omelet to a cutting board, it should be sliced into four even wedges. Serve

Dietary Composition: Caloric Intake: 250, Quantity of Protein: 15g, Quantity of fat: 15g, Quantity of Carbohydrates: 5g, Quantity of Fiber: 4g

17. Morning Couscous

Readiness Time: 5-9 minutes Time needed to cook: 23 minutes Quantity of Meals: 4

Required Material:

- Milk of soy: three mugs
- Cinnamon: Only one stick
- Couscous, whole wheat, uncooked: 1 cup
- Currants: 1/4 cup
- Crushed butter: 4 teaspoons
- Apricots: 1/2 cup
- Brown sugar: 6 teaspoons
- Salt: use a pinch to taste

Step-By-Step Procedure:

1. Put the soy milk and cinnamon stick in a saucepan and cook until the milk is hot.
2. Instead of letting the mixture boil, heat it for three minutes at a time or until little bubbles appear on the inside of the pan.
3. Put the couscous inside a pan together with the currants, apricots, salt, and sugar once you've removed it from the heat.
4. Set the pan aside, covered, for 20 mins. Eliminate the cinnamon stick from the pan.

5. Serve soup in four bowls, and garnish each with a half-teaspoon of sugar and a teaspoon of butter that has been melted

Dietary Composition: Caloric Intake: 170, Quantity of Protein: 4g, Quantity of fat: 1g, Quantity of Carbohydrates: 37g, Quantity of Fiber: 3g

18. Multigrain Toast with Grilled Vegetables

Readiness Time: 7 minutes Time needed to cook: 5 minutes Quantity of Meals: 6

Required Material:

- Eggplant: Half
- Yellow, red and green pepper: One and 1/2
- Multigrain bread: 6 slices
- Goat cheese: 3 ounces
- Squash: Half
- One teaspoon of EVO oil
- Zucchini: 1/2
- fresh bouquet of marjoram: One-fourth
- Cracked black pepper for seasoning

Step-By-Step Procedure:

1. Slice the eggplant, zucchini, and squash into 1-inch long pieces, split the peppers in half lengthwise.
2. Prepare a hot grill. Fork-tender veggies may be achieved by tossing them in oil and grilling them.
3. Cut all the veggies into big pieces. (The vegetables may be cooked the night before; simply store them in the refrigerator and reheat them before serving.)
4. Grill the bread, then remove it from the flame and top it with your favorite veggies. Black pepper, minced marjoram, and cheese are sprinkled over top.

Dietary Composition: Caloric Intake: 200, Quantity of Protein: 6g, Quantity of

Carbohydrates: 30g, Quantity of fat: 7g, Quantity of Fiber: 5g

19. Pancetta on Baguette

Readiness Time: 5-7 minutes Time needed to cook: 4 minutes Quantity of Meals: 6

Required Material:

- A loaf baguette
- EVO oil: 1/2–1 tsp
- Pancetta (ham, prosciutto): 6 ounces
- Cantaloupe, medium-diced: 1/4
- Cheese, type goat: 3 ounces
- Honeydew melon: 1-quarter
- Fresh-cracked black pepper

Step-By-Step Procedure:

1. Turn on the broiler and set the temperature to medium-high.
2. Baguette halves should be placed on a baking sheet after being cut lengthwise in half.
3. After coating each side with oil, lightly toast the bread.
4. Pancetta should be sliced as thinly as paper and then arranged in narrow strips on the baguette pieces.
5. Broil it for 1 minute, keeping a careful watch on it to ensure it doesn't burn.
6. Cantaloupe and honeydew may be mixed together in a small dish while the baguette bakes.

7. When the baguette is done, take it out of the oven and lay it on a platter. Add some goat cheese and ground black pepper on top.
8. Add a little of the melon mixture on the top and serve

Dietary Composition: Caloric Intake: 400, Quantity of Protein: 5g, Quantity of fat: 30g, Quantity of Carbohydrates: 40g

20. Quiche Wrapped in Prosciutto

Readiness Time: 6-8 minutes Time needed to cook: 15 minutes Quantity of Meals: 8

Required Material:

- Four slices prosciutto, halved
- Egg: 2 only white + 1 whole
- Rosemary: 1/2 tsp and a little more for garnishing
- Greek yoghur, low fat: 3 tbsp
- Black olives: 1 tbsp.
- Pepper and salt, a pich of each

Step-By-Step Procedure:

1. Adjust your oven temperature to 400 degrees F and grease a muffin tin.
2. Arrange the prosciutto so that each of the tray's eight cups can accommodate one slice.
3. In a medium dish, mix the egg whites and whole egg by whisking them together.
4. Whisk in oil, pepper, salt, rosemary, and yogurt until smooth.
5. Cover and bake, about 15 mins, after you have spread the mixture equally among the prepared cups.
6. Rosemary season for trim.

Dietary Composition: Caloric Intake: 500, Quantity of Protein: 20g, Quantity of fat: 35g, Quantity of Carbohydrates: 20g, Quantity of Fiber: 2g

21. Sautéed Dandelion Toast

Readiness Time: 15-18 minutes Time needed to cook: 10 minutes Quantity of Meals: 2

Required Material:

- Dandelion: two bunches
- Shallot or green onion: Two medium or One small
- Anchovies fillets: Two
- Two minced garlic cloves
- Red pepper flakes: 1 pinch
- A lemon, rind and juice
- A little sprinkling of honey.
- Salt, Olive oil and Pepper, use to taste
- Almonds that are chopped and roasted: a handful
- The crumbling of a mild, spreadable sheep's milk cheese (similar in consistency to goat's milk)

Step-By-Step Procedure:

1. Dandelion leaves should be stripped from the stem before use. If you don't have a knife on hand, you may use your thumb and fingers to pry off the leaves from the green rod at the branch's base. Dandelion greens should be cut roughly but the stems neatly.
2. Get a skillet hot. Add at least 2 tablespoons of olive oil to serve as a binder. Toss in some salt, pepper, olive oil, anchovies, and onion rings (or shallots), then roast for about 5 minutes. Soak the chopped onion and anchovy in the olive oil to make them more tender.
3. Add some chopped dandelion greens. Stir in some salt and pepper to taste. Dressing through is a must if you want to improve the flavor.
4. After mixing in the zest of half a lemon, bake for 5 minutes. When the stems are soft but still have a little crunch, they are at their best. Now is the moment to give the mixture a quick taste to see whether the flavors mesh well together.

5. The stalk and onion mix need dandelion leaves added to it. We could use a little extra salt. Dandelion leaves may be cooked to a more palatable consistency and lessen their bitterness by being stirred at regular intervals.
6. When finished, sprinkle over some lemon juice and honey. To finish, sprinkle some pepper flakes and the remaining lemon peel over the dish.
7. Combine with tangy sheep cheese and roasted almonds.

Dietary Composition: Caloric Intake: 100, Quantity of Protein: 3g, Quantity of Carbohydrates: 12g, Quantity of fat: 3g, Quantity of Fiber: 4g

22. Yogurt Pancakes

Readiness Time: 5 minutes Time needed to cook: 4 minutes Quantity of Meals: 5

Required Material:

- Whole-wheat Mix pancake
- Yogurt: A cup's worth
- Baking powder and soda: 2 tbsps. (one each)
- Eggs 3
- Skim milk: One cup
- Extra-virgin olive oil: 1/2 teaspoon

Step-By-Step Procedure:

1. Mix all the ingredients: Whole-wheat mix, yogurt, baking powder and soda, skim milk, and eggs. Blend together by stirring for a few minutes.
2. Warm up a skillet with olive oil.
3. Cook for two mins, or until the top of the pancake is bubbling, after adding a quarter cup of batter to the heated pan.
4. Brown the underside first, then flip and repeat on the other side.
5. Pancakes hot, milk without any fat or two tablespoons of light maple syrup, served all together.

Dietary Composition: Caloric Intake: 250, Quantity of Protein: 10g, Quantity of fat: 10g, Quantity of Carbohydrates: 30g, Quantity of Fiber: 2g

SALADS

23. Arugula Salad, Figs and Shaved Cheese

Readiness Time: 10-13 minutes Time needed to cook: 0 minutes Quantity of Meals: 6

Required Material:

- Honey: one tablespoon
- Balsamic vinegar: three tablespoons
- Monin Mustard: one teaspoon
- Salt: one teaspoon
- Garlic: 1
- A pinch of spice (pepper)
- Olive oil pure: 2/3 of a cup
- Arugula leaves: 5 cups
- Graviera cheese: a quarter cup
- 12 fresh (ripe) fruits figs;
- Nuts, around 1 cup

Step-By-Step Procedure:

1. Mix the honey, mustard, vinegar, garlic, salt, and pepper in a large basin.
2. Slowly and completely incorporate the oil.
3. Toss the arugula and figs together. To ensure that the salad is well covered with the dressing, combine the two.

4. Add some cheese and nuts to your salad and serve.

Dietary Composition: Caloric Intake: 150, Quantity of Protein: 6g, Quantity of fat: 10g, Quantity of fat: 5g, Quantity of Carbohydrates: 15g, Quantity of Fiber: 3g

24. Bulgur Salad

Readiness Time: 6-7 minutes Time needed to cook: 20 minutes Quantity of Meals: 4

Required Material:

- Butter, unsalted: one tablespoon
- Extra-virgin olive oil: 2 tablespoons total split
- Bulgur: 2 mugs
- Salt: A quarter of a teaspoon
- Water: four mugs
- Cucumber: 1
- Black olives: a handful
- Vinegar from a red wine: 2 teaspoons
- Dill: 1-quarter cup

Step-By-Step Procedure:

1. Put a saucepan on the stove, add a little bit of butter and a tablespoon of olive oil.
2. Toasted bulgur turns out crunchy and golden brown from being fried in oil.
3. To a sauce pan, add the salt and 4 cups of water.
4. For around 20 minutes on low heat, covered, you should be able to absorb all the liquid.
5. Combine the diced cucumber, dill, olives, red wine vinegar, and olive oil in a bowl and set aside.
6. Put it on top of the bulgur before serve

Dietary Composition: Caloric Intake: 250, Quantity of Protein: 10g, Quantity of Carbohydrates: 50g, Quantity of fat: 7g, Quantity of Fiber: 8g

25. Chickpea Salad with Yogurt Dressing

Readiness Time: 10-13 minutes Time needed to cook: 0 minutes Quantity of Meals: 4

Required Material:

Dressing

- Squeezed-fresh lemon juice: One teaspoon
- Greek yogurt, without fat: One cup
- Cayenne pepper: one-fourth of a teaspoon
- Curry powder: one and a half teaspoons

Salad:

- Chickpeas, already drained and rinsed: 2 cans (15-ounce)
- Diced red apple: 1 cup
- Celery: half cup
- Walnuts and onion: 1/4 cup (each)
- Raisin:1/3 cup
- Parsley: 1/2 cup
- Lemon: Two slices

Step-By-Step Procedure:

1. Unite together lemon juice, yogurt, cayenne pepper, and curry powder.
2. Toss the chickpeas with the apple, walnuts, green onions, raisins, and parsley. Salt and pepper to taste, then gently mix in the dressing.
3. Put lemon slices on the plate as a garnish.

Dietary Composition: Caloric Intake: 280, Quantity of fat: 11g, Quantity of Carbohydrates: 26g, Quantity of Protein: 14g, Quantity of Fiber: 5g

26. Creamy Caesar Salad

Readiness Time: 5 minutes Time needed to cook: 6 minutes Quantity of Meals: 6

Required Material:

- Garlic: 2 cloves
- Mustard: 1 Tbsp.
- Egg yolks: 3
- Worcestershire sauce: 3 tablespoons
- Anchovy fillets: 2
- Parmesan cheese: 1/2 mug
- Squeezed lemon juice: Two tbsps.
- Salt: half tsp
- Pepper: a pinch
- Olive oil: one cup
- Romaine lettuce: one head
- Cooked bacon: half a cup
- Croutons: one cup
- Water: one tbsp

Step-By-Step Procedure:

1. Combine the garlic, egg yolks, mustard, Worcestershire sauce, anchovy, cheese, lemon juice, salt, and water. Whisk until you have a thick dressing.
2. Incorporate oil gradually while the processor is running to get a smooth mixture. You may adjust with spices.
3. Add the remaining lemon juice with the lettuce in a large bowl.
4. Add enough dressing so that the lettuce is evenly coated (or more if you want a creamier salad). Add the remaining Parmesan cheese to the salad. Serve.

Dietary Composition: Caloric Intake: 500, Quantity of fat: 30g, Quantity of Protein: 15g, Quantity of Carbohydrates: 30g, Quantity of Fiber: 4g

27. Cucumber and Dill Dressing

Readiness Time: 5 minutes Time needed to cook: 0 minutes Quantity of Meals: 4

Required Material:

- English cucumber: 1/2
- Salt: 3/4 tsp
- Greek yogurt, strained: 1/2 cup
- Whole milk: A quarter cup
- Mayonnaise: a half-teaspoon
- Fresh lemon juice: Two teaspoons
- A small onion (white part only), trimmed, delicately cut
- A clove of garlic, skinned and minced
- Fresh dill: Two tablespoons
- Pepper.

Step-By-Step Procedure:

1. Strain the cucumber over a fine-mesh bowl and add salt. Wait 30 minutes. Squeeze the cucumber to remove any excess liquid.
2. Unite the cucumber with other components. Stir the ingredients well to combine them.
3. The dressing may be stored for up to a week in an airtight container.

Dietary Composition: Caloric Intake: 25, Quantity of fat: 0g, Quantity of Carbohydrates: 4g, Quantity of Protein: 0g

28. Dandelion Greens

Readiness Time: 5 minutes Time needed to cook: 8-10 minutes Quantity of Meals: 6

Required Material:

- Dandelion greens: weighing 4 pounds
- Oil and lemon juice: Half cup of each
- Season to taste with salt and pepper.

Step-By-Step Procedure:

1. The stems of daisy greens should be removed and cleaned before eating.
2. Bring a big saucepan of water to a boil, then add the greens.

3. Greens need approximately 8-10 minutes of cooking over high heat to become soft; once done, they should be removed, drained, and served.
4. Mix up some olive oil, lemon juice, salt, and pepper, then dress the salad leaves. Serve hot or cold; pair with grilled fish; or enjoy on their own with crisp bread, briny olives, and salty feta.
5. Mince some fresh garlic and sprinkle it on top.

Dietary Composition: Caloric Intake: 41, Quantity of fat: 0.5 g, Quantity of Carbohydrates: 7 g, Quantity of Fiber: 3 g, Quantity of Protein: 3 g

29. Greek Salad

Readiness Time: 5 minutes Time needed to cook: 0 minutes Quantity of Meals: 4

Required Material:

- Only juice of lemon: One
- High-quality olive oil: six tablespoons
- Black pepper: ground for seasoning
- Feta cheese: One cup
- Onion: 1
- Oregano: one teaspoon
- Romaine lettuce: One head
- Sweet red and green pepper: 2
- Cucumber: one
- Tomato slices: two
- Olives, black: One can

Step-By-Step Procedure:

1. Lime juice, olive oil, black pepper, and oregano should be mixed in a small bowl.
2. Using a large bowl, toss together the lettuce, peppers, cucumber, tomato, onion, and cheese.
3. Toss the salad in this bowl to combine it with the dressing.

Dietary Composition: Caloric Intake: 300, Quantity of fat: 22g, Quantity of Carbohydrates: 16g, Quantity of Protein: 8g

30. Grilled Eggplant Salad

Readiness Time: 10-14 minutes Time needed to cook: 40 minutes Quantity of Meals: 4

Required Material:

- Salt: 2 tbsp plus more for seasoning
- Tomatoes: 2 or 3 (depending on size
- Eggplant: one
- Garlic: 2 cloves
- A sprinkling of parsley
- Oregano: One Tbsp
- Evo oil: 1-quarter cup

Step-By-Step Procedure:

1. Diced eggplant should have a thickness of around 1/4 inch, falling between between being too thin and too thick. Put egg plant dice in a salt bath and use a plate to weigh it down; fill a big mixing bowl or saucepan with water and add 2 tablespoons of salt; mix to blend.
2. Leave it alone for twenty to thirty minutes. Make sure they are thoroughly submerged by stirring them around every so often in the salty water.
3. Dice some tomatoes and set them aside in a basin. Parsley, garlic, salt, pepper, oregano, and a couple of tablespoons of olive oil should be combined and put aside.

4. Turn the heat up high and light the grill. When is ready, spray it with vegetable oil or wipe it down.
5. Use your hands to swiftly brush olive oil onto the bottom of each egg plant slice after you have drained and dried. Place in rows over the whole grill, starting in the upper left corner of the back.
6. After grilling the eggplant slices, brush (or spray) the upward-facing sides with olive oil. It should take around 6-8 minutes on the grill for the edges and center to soften. Keep a careful watch on them while you let each side cook for a few minutes to ensure equal cooking and oil absorption.
7. Repeat the process of brushing with olive oil, flipping, grilling for a few more minutes, and finishing with a final coating of oil.
8. Keep on grill for a minute or two more, then remove and lay to a serving dish.
9. Spread the chopped tomato mixture over the eggplant rounds, sprinkle with the oregano, and serve with crusty bread.

Dietary Composition: Caloric Intake: 30, Quantity of fat: 0.5g, Quantity of Carbohydrates: 5.9g, Quantity of Fiber: 2.7g, Quantity of Protein: 1.2g

31. Grilled Tofu with Mediterranean Salad

Readiness Time: 10-13 minutes Time needed to cook: 35 minutes Quantity of Meals: 4

Required Material:

- Evo oil: 3 tbsp
- Extra-firm tofu: 14 ounces
- Oregano: two tsp
- Garlic: 3
- Mediterranean Chopped Salad
- Sea salt: ½ tsp.
- Freshly pepper
- Kalamata olives: 1/4 mug
- Cucumber: just 1 cup
- Lemon juice: just 1/4 mug
- Tomatoes: 2 medium

- Scallions, parsley (chopped): 1-quarter cup
- White-wine vinegar: one tbsp
- Freshly ground pepper
- Salt of sea: 1-quarter tsp

Step-By-Step Procedure:

1. Start the barbecue. Mix extra virgin olive oil, lemon juice, oregano, garlic, salt, and pepper in a small dish. Use 2 tablespoons for basting.
2. Rinse tofu in cold water after draining. Dry with paper towels. Eight 12-inch-thick tofu slices are put on a transparent dish.
3. Toss tofu in lemon juice marinade. It is best served cold.
4. Meanwhile, mix the salad ingredients in a medium bowl. Set aside.
5. Prepare the grill rack with oil. Drain and cut marinated tofu.
6. Baste the tofu with marinade, grill for 4 minutes per side.
7. Serve with a cool salad.

Dietary Composition: Caloric Intake: 218, Quantity of fat: 14g, Quantity of Carbohydrates: 10g, Quantity of Protein: 12g, Quantity of Fiber: 3g.

32. Israeli Couscous with Currants

Readiness Time: 15-18 minutes Time needed to cook: 20 minutes Quantity of Meals: 12 side-dishes

Required Material:

- Green onions, one bundle
- Israeli (pearl) couscous: 3 cups
- Margarine or spread: 2 tablespoons
- Chicken stock and water: 1+2 cups
- Ground allspice 1/4 teaspoons
- Pecans: 3/4 cup
- Dried currants: 1/2 cup
- Leaves mint plants pressed: 1/2 mug

Step-By-Step Procedure:

1. Cut one piece of the half-inch measure white and green of1 bunch of onions.
2. Slice the onions into and divide the various pieces of onion.
3. In a 4-quart saucepot, melt 2 tablespoons of margarine or spread.
4. Cook for another 3 minutes, after adding the white and light green onions.
5. Sauté the Israeli (pearl) couscous for 7–9 minutes, or until most of the grains are opaque and tender, turning often.
6. Two cups of water, one cup of chicken stock, one-fourth teaspoon of ground allspice, salt, and pepper should be brought to a boil in a large saucepan before adding the couscous. Cover, and cook for 8-10 minutes.
7. Put an end to cooking the couscous.
8. Mix roasted pecans with currants, pressed mint leaves, and saved sliced green onions.
9. Serve.

Dietary Composition: Caloric Intake: Caloric Intake: 160, Quantity of fat: 1g, Quantity of Carbohydrates: 32g, Quantity of Protein: 5g, Quantity of Fiber: 1g

33. Kalamata Olive Dressing

Readiness Time: 5 minutes Time needed to cook: 0 minutes Quantity of Meals: 4

Required Material:

- Minced red onions: One-fourth cup
- Crushed garlic: 1 clove
- Kalamata olives, pitted: One-half cup
- Sun-dried tomatoes (drained from their olive oil packaging): 2
- Dried oregano: A total of half a teaspoon
- Red wine vinegar: 2 tablespoons
- Balsamic vinegar: 1 tablespoon
- Black pepper: 1/2 teaspoon
- (Extra-Virgin) olive oil: 2/3 cup
- Dijon mustard: 1 tsp

Step-By-Step Procedure:

1. Combine all ingredients in a food processor and blend for a few minutes.
2. Keep the dressing in the fridge.

Dietary Composition: Caloric Intake: 119, Quantity of fat: 13g, Quantity of Carbohydrates: 2g, Quantity of Protein: 0g

34. Lemon Orzo Fish Salad

Readiness Time: 5 minutes Time needed to cook: 0 minutes Serve 4

Required Material:

- Orzo pasta, uncooked: 12 ounces
- Finely minced scallions: One cup
- Luscious, ripe raisins: One-half cup
- Juice from 1/4 cup of lemon
- Pure olive oil: 1/3 cup
- Zing Lemon Extract: One Tablespoon
- Both the salt and pepper we use are freshly ground.
- Two fish-filled: 12-ounce jars

Step-By-Step Procedure:

1. To establish how long the orzo should be cooked, use the direction on the package.
2. Place the orzo in a bowl and mix all the components on the list.
3. Season with salt and pepper before serving.

Dietary Composition: Caloric Intake: 459, Quantity of fat: 15g, Quantity of Carbohydrates: 58g, Quantity of Protein: 17g, Quantity of Fiber: 4g

35. Macedonia Serving of Mixed Greens

Readiness Time: 10-15 minutes Time needed to cook: 0 minutes Quantity of Meals: 6

Required Material:

- One lime (at room temperature)
- Cubed peaches or nectarines: One cup
- Strawberries, or a mixture of your preferred fruit: 1 cup
- Grapes, seedless: one cup's worth (green, red, or a mix).
- Melon balls, honeydew melon balls, watermelon balls, etc., to make: 1 cup.
- Sugar (optional, although it helps bring out the juice): 1-quarter cup
- At your choice: Red wine (attempt a Zinfandel for a rich, peppery impact, a Pinot Noir for a lighter desire): ½ cup or Alcohol (Fabulous Marnier, kirsch, or amaretto): 2 tablespoons or Squeezed orange: ½ cup

Step-By-Step Procedure:

1. After carefully rolling the lemon down the counter, cut it in half across the width.
2. Be cautious not to crush or pound the organic food as you gently stir in the remaining product and then squeeze each lemon quarter over the top.
3. Sprinkle some sugar and then incorporate the liquid element of your choice (wine or freshly squeezed orange juice or alcohol). Give it a little toss.
4. Ten minutes at room temperature is the least, and sixty is the maximum, before serving.

Dietary Composition: Caloric Intake: 152, Quantity of fat: 10g, Quantity of Carbohydrates: 11g, Quantity of Protein: 5g, Quantity of Fiber: 4 g

36. Mediterranean Quinoa Salad

Readiness Time: 8-10 minutes Time needed to cook: 20 minutes Serve 4

Required Material:

- Mashed garlic: One clove
- Water: 2 cups
- chicken broth: 2 cubes
- Raw quinoa: one cup
- Kalamata olives, chopped: 1/2 cup
- Big sliced red onion: 1
- Huge breasts of chicken, cooked: Two
- Green sweet pepper: 1
- Feta cheese, crumbled: Half cup
- Aromatic herbs (parsley and chives): One-fourth cup of each
- Salt: Half a teaspoon
- Oil: a quarter of a cup
- Pure lemon, juice: 2/3 mug
- Vinegar, balsamic: one tablespoon's worth

Step-By-Step Procedure:

1. Unite onion, garlic, water, and bouillon cubes in a skillet and bring them to a simmer (20 mins.).
2. Add the quinoa, mix, and simmer, covered. Cooked quinoa should be transferred, after eliminating the garlic, to a large bowl.
3. Toss the chicken, sweet pepper, chives, parsley, feta cheese, sea salt, oil, balsamic vinegar, and lemon juice together. Ready to be eaten or chilled

Dietary Composition: Caloric Intake: 263, Quantity of fat: 11.2g, Quantity of Carbohydrates: 32.8g, Quantity of Protein: 8.1g, Quantity of Fiber: 4.8g

37. Potato Salad with Lemon

Readiness Time: 15-18 minutes Time needed to cook: 30 minutes Quantity of Meals: 6

Required Material:

- Yukon gold potatoes, large: 6
- Salt: 1 and half tsp
- Pepper: a pinch
- Oil of olive: 1/2 cup (Extra-virgin)
- Dijon mustard: 1-quarter cup
- Capers, drained and chopped: 2 tbsp
- Red wine vinegar: 1/4 mug
- Use fresh parsley: Two tablespoons
- Scallions: 3
- Fresh dill: Half mug
- Lemon, only fresh juice squeezed: just 1 tbsp

Step-By-Step Procedure:

1. Potatoes may be cooked by bringing a big saucepan filled with water to a boil over medium heat, adding the potatoes, and then covering and cooking them until they are soft.
2. Give it 30 minutes to cook.
3. Cool the potatoes for at least 10 minutes before attempting to peel them. Cut the potatoes into small cubes.
4. In a large bowl, combine the other ingredients and blend until smooth.
5. Incorporate the potatoes by tossing them into the dressing.
6. Salads are best served warm or at room temperature.

Dietary Composition: Caloric Intake: 140, Quantity of fat: 10g, Quantity of Carbohydrates: 11g, Quantity of Protein: 2g

38. Slashed Beet and Arugula Salad

Readiness Time: 5 minutes Time needed to cook: 45-50 minutes Serve 4

Required Material:

- Beet: 1
- Orange juice: Three tablespoons
- Powder spices (Salt, mustard, pepper): quantity to taste
- Liquids (White wine vinegar and EVO oil): One Tbsp of each
- Newly-cut bouquets of arugula: 2
- Feta cheddar: one cup
- Oranges, type navel: Two

Step-By-Step Procedure:

1. Raise the oven's temperature to 450 degrees Fahrenheit to get ready for the cook. Protect the beet by wrapping it with foil. Cooking time for beets in the oven is around 45-50 minutes.
2. Once the beets have cooled for a few minutes after coming off the grill, remove the foil and use a paper towel to peel off the skin. Beets are cut into fourths and put away. Squeeze the juice of one orange into a small bowl and stir in the vinegar, mustard, and olive oil.
3. It's recommended that you divide the arugula, beets, oranges, and crumbled feta into four separate serving plates. Present it for consumption after adding dressing.

Dietary Composition: Caloric Intake: 207, Quantity of fat: 12.5g, Quantity of Carbohydrates: 16.4g, Quantity of Protein: 7.8g

39. Spinach Salad with Apples and Mint

Readiness Time: 10-12 minutes Time needed to cook: 0 minutes Quantity of Meals: 4

Required Material:

- Pure olive oil: A third of a cup; Finely chopped mint leaves, fresh: Ten
- Orange, set juice aside: one
- Peeled and cut big grapefruit: 1 (set aside the juice)
- 100% pure lime juice: 1 tbsp
- Salt: 3-quarter tsp
- Pepper: One-quarter of a tsp
- Baby spinach: about 4 cups
- Red and green apples, peeled, cored, and cut thinly: 2
- Red onion: 1/3 mug
- Celery stick: one

Step-By-Step Procedure:

1. Use a blender or food processor to thoroughly combine the oil and mint. Set aside to allow the oil to absorb the mint taste.
2. Orange juice, grapefruit juice, lime juice, salt, pepper, and olive oil infused with mint should all be combined in a big dish. Prepare the salad by slicing the apple, onion, and celery. Dress the salad and toss before serving.
3. The salad and dressing need spinach back in them. Serve with a garnish of orange and grapefruit segments.

Dietary Composition: Caloric Intake: 183, Quantity of fat: 6.3g, Quantity of Carbohydrates: 28.2g, Quantity of Protein: 3.7g, Quantity of Fiber: 4.7g

40. Strawberry Feta Salad Balsamic Dressing

Readiness Time: 5 minutes Time needed to cook: 0 minutes Quantity of Meals: 4

Required Material:

- Mustard seeds (Djon): 1 tsp.
- Balsamic vinegar: three tbsp worth
- Garlic segment, peeled and minced: One
- Salad greens: Four cups
- Ripe strawberries that have been hulled and cut in half: one pint

- Feta cheese: one and a half cups
- Salt - Pepper: use to like

Step-By-Step Procedure:

1. To make the dressing, put all the ingredients in a small bowl and whisk them together until you have a uniform consistency: mustard, vinegar, garlic, oil, salt, and pepper.
2. In a large basin, toss together the salad greens and dressing.
3. To serve, arrange the salad in a serving dish and dot with goat cheese and strawberries. If there is extra dressing, serve it beside the salad.

Dietary Composition: Caloric Intake: 220, Quantity of fat: 10g, Quantity of Carbohydrates: 20g, Quantity of Protein: 6g

41. **Tomato Salad with Fried Feta**

Readiness Time: 30 minutes Time needed to cook: 1-2 minutes Quantity of Meals: 4

Required Material:

- Egg, just 1
- Flour of any kind: 1-quarter cup
- Whole milk: 1 teaspoon
- Feta cheese, cubed into 12-inch pieces: 1 1/2 cups
- Lemon juice, fresh: (1 tbsp)
- The same quantity of Djón mustard, salt, honey: One tsp

- Virgin olive oil: 1 2/3 cups
- Balsamic vinegar, 1 tbsp
- Cinnamon and Pepper (each): 1/4 teaspoon
- Dry Oregano, 2 Teaspoons
- Ripe tomatoes:2
- Salad greens: Four cups
- Kalamata olives: half a cup
- A tiny red onion

Step-By-Step Procedure:

1. In a small bowl, whisk together the egg and milk. To a separate, smaller bowl, add the flour.
2. After immersing the feta cubes in the egg mixture, dredge them in flour. Shake out any excess flour.
3. The feta should be chilled in the fridge for at least 30 minutes after being dredged.
4. Squeeze the lemons and add the juice, oil (2/3 cup), mustard, vinegar, honey, oregano, salt, and pepper to a small jar with a cover.
5. Close the jar after shaking it hard to combine the dressing.
6. The remaining oil should be heated for one minute in a medium nonstick frying pan over medium heat.
7. Fry the feta for approximately 20 to 30 seconds on each side, or until it is gently browned.
8. Put the feta on a paper towel-lined pan to catch any oil that may have accumulated.
9. Combine the salad, onions, olives, and tomatoes in a large serving dish.
10. Before putting it on the salad, shake the dressing.
11. Toss the ingredients together.

Dietary Composition: Caloric Intake: 250, Quantity of fat: 17g, Quantity of Carbohydrates: 11g, Quantity of Protein: 8g, Quantity of Fiber: 2g

42. Tuna Salad with Toasted Pine Nuts

Readiness Time: 5 minutes Time needed to cook: 0 minutes Quantity of Meals: 4

Required Material:

- olive-oil-packed of tuna: (5-ounce) 1 can
- Fresh chives, chopped: about 3 tablespoons
- One shallot
- Fresh tarragon, chopped: (1 tbsp)
- Celery stalk, cleaned and chopped: 1
- Mayonnaise: about 2–3 tbsp
- Dijon Mustard: 1 tsp
- Salt: 1,25 g
- Pepper: 1/8 tsp
- Toasted pine nuts: 1/4 cup of

Step-By-Step Procedure:

1. For a medium bowl, combine the tuna, shallot, chives, tarragon, and celery.
2. Combine the mayonnaise, mustard, salt, and pepper in a separate small bowl.
3. Combine the mayonnaise mixture with the canned tuna.
4. Add some pine nuts, please.
5. Serve chilled or at room temperature.

Dietary Composition: Caloric Intake: 320, Quantity of fat: 19g, Quantity of Protein: 27g, Quantity of Carbohydrates: 6g, Quantity of Fiber: 2g

43. Warm Lentil Salad

Readiness Time: 10-13 minutes Time needed to cook: 9 minutes Quantity of Meals: 4

Required Material:

- High-quality olive oil: Three tablespoons
- Leeks, cut thinly:1 1/2 cups
- Crumbled feta cheese: one-fourth cup
- Mustard: 2 teaspoons
- Cooked lentils: Two cups
- Red grapes: (halved one and a half cups)

- Chopped roasted pistachios: 1-quarter mug
- Parsley and mint, both good chopping: 6 tbsp (The same quantity of each)
- Sherry Vinegar: Two tbsp

Step-By-Step Procedure:

1. In a small pan, warm the oil of olive. Toss in the leeks and cook until translucent and soft, approximately 9 minutes, turning often.
2. Remove the pan from the heat and add the mustard and sherry, stirring to combine.
3. The lentils, grapes, pistachios, mint, parsley, sea salt, and pepper should be added to the leek mixture after it has been mixed. Cover in some feta and enjoy yourself.

Dietary Composition: Caloric Intake: 250, Quantity of fat: 12g, Quantity of Carbohydrates: 28g, Quantity of Protein: 10g, Quantity of Fiber: 8g

44. Warm Mushroom Salad

Readiness Time: 15-19 minutes Time needed to cook: 20 minutes Quantity of Meals: 4

Required Material:

- Cremini and king mushrooms: 4 mugs (Two of each)
- EVO oil: 2/3 mug
- Peeled and crushed garlic: Six cloves
- Rosemary sprig: 1 tsp
- Bay leaves: Two
- Fresh thyme leaves: one teaspoon
- Season with salt, pepper: 1 teaspoon
- Mustard: just 1 tsp.
- Balsamic vinegar: Two Tbsp.
- Lemon juice: One fresh tablespoon
- Salad greens: about four cups' worth, washed and dried
- Pumpkin Seeds: 1/4 mug
- Goat cheese, crumbled: Half a cup
- Onion chunks: One-fourth cup

Step-By-Step Procedure:

1. In a large cast-iron skillet, heat a third of a cup of oil (30 seconds). Add the mushrooms, garlic, bay leaves, rosemary, thyme, 1/2 teaspoon of salt, 1/4 teaspoon of pepper, and the rest of the herbs. Simmer the mushrooms for 20 minutes, stirring occasionally, and then remove and discard the bay leaves.

2. In a small jar with a lid, combine the remaining dressing ingredients and shake firmly until everything is uniformly distributed.

3. In a large bowl, combine the salad greens with the dressing. After plating the greens, split the heated mushrooms and place them on top.

4. Add pumpkin seeds, grated cheese, and fresh, crunchy onions to the salad. Salads should be topped with the leftover dressing. They're delicious served either hot or cold.

Dietary Composition: Caloric Intake: 300, Quantity of fat: 8g, Quantity of Carbohydrates: 28g, Quantity of Protein: 10g, Quantity of Fiber: 4g

SOUP AND STEW

45. Artichoke Soup

Readiness Time: 20-23 minutes Time needed to cook: 55 minutes Quantity of Meals: 8

Required Material:

- Fresh giant artichokes (already clean): 18
- Fresh lemon juice: 6 tablespoons
- Virgin olive oil: A quarter cup of
- Big potatoes: 3
- Salt: 1 1/2 teaspoons
- Pepper: 1/2 teaspoon
- Leeks, cut and washed: 6
- Veggie broth: 10 cups
- Greek yogurt with a sprinkle of chopped fresh chives: Half a cup (each)

Step-By-Step Procedure:

1. In a large dish, combine the artichoke hearts, three tablespoons of lemon juice, and enough water to cover them.
2. In a big saucepan warm the oil for 30 seconds. Add the leeks, along with a pinch of salt and a pinch of pepper. Ten minutes should be enough time for the leeks to soften.
3. After they have been drained, add the artichokes, potatoes, and stock to the

leeks. The soup should be brought to a boil. Add the remaining salt and pepper.
4. Get ready to wait about 45 minutes. Put the saucepan down and turn off the burner.
5. Carefully blend the soup until it reaches a silky-smooth consistency.
6. To taste, add more salt and pepper and the rest of the lemon juice.
7. Put a dollop of yogurt and some chives on top of each bowl of soup.

Dietary Composition: Caloric Intake: 70, Quantity of fat: 2g, Quantity of Carbohydrates: 10g, Quantity of Protein: 3g, Quantity of Fiber: 2g

46. Bean and Cabbage Soup

Readiness Time: 20-23 minutes Time needed to cook: 45 minutes Quantity of Meals: 6

Required Material:

- Extra-Virgin Olive Oil: 1-quarter Cup
- Onion chopped, 1/2 cup
- Tomatoes: 14.5 ounces or 1 can
- Carrot and Stalks celery: (each) Two
- Beans, type cannellini: A can
- Water: 8 mugs
- Baked ham: a half-pound
- Parsley, springs: 6
- Sage, dried: 1-quarter tsp
- Chopped green cabbage: Six cups
- Yukon potatoes: a half-pound
- Instant polenta: a quarter-cup
- Bay leaf: One
- Pepper and salt of the sea

Step-By-Step Procedure:

1. Extra virgin olive oil warm is used to sauté the onions, celery, and carrots for approximately 7 mins.

2. Then, stir in the tomatoes, sage, parsley, and bay leaf, and boil everything together for 10 minutes.
3. After adding water and mixing, bring to a boil.
4. Beans, ham, cabbage, and potatoes may be added after the heat has been lowered.
5. It should take around 20 minutes to cook until the potatoes are soft.
6. Add polenta and stir; cook (five mins.) at a low flame before adding salt and pepper to taste.
7. Dish up in the cups of soup.

Dietary Composition: Caloric Intake: 140, Quantity of fat: 2.5g, Quantity of Carbohydrates: 24g, Quantity of Protein: 6g, Quantity of Fiber: 7g

47. Beet Soup

Readiness Time: 25-27 minutes Time needed to cook: 2 hours Quantity of Meals: 6

Required Material:

- Olive oil: One-quarter mug
- Onion: Three medium
- Vegetables (Beets, Carrots, Potatoes, Celery stalks):
- White cabbage: two cups
- Garlic cloves: 3
- Tomato purée: 1 cup
- Parsley, fresh, chopped: 1/2 cups
- Meat stock (beef or veal): 6-8 cups
- Salt
- Red wine vinegar: 1/4 cup
- Pepper
- Dill fresh, chopped: 1/2 cup

Step-By-Step Procedure:

1. Start the oven temperature up to reach 450 degrees F. Oil the beets with 1 tbsp.
2. After wrapping in foil, insert the tin inside the oven. Wait 45 minutes, or until a fork can easily penetrate the center.
3. Peel the beets gently using the back of the knife. Slice the beets in half.

4. Warm the remaining oil for 30 seconds in a big saucepan.
5. Once onions, garlic, carrots, and celery have been added, they should be cooked for 15 mins.
6. Add cabbage, tomato, parsley, and beets and continue cooking for another 5 mins.
7. Turn the heat up, add stock and potatoes, and bring the soup to a boil.
8. Boil until potatoes are soft, about 45 mins to an hour.
9. Combine the vinegar and dill, and then serve.

Dietary Composition: Caloric Intake: 100, Quantity of fat: 0g, Quantity of Carbohydrates: 20g, Quantity of Protein: 5g, Quantity of Fiber: 3g

48. Carrot-Thyme Soup

Readiness Time: 25-28 minutes Time needed to cook: 1 hour and 25 minutes Quantity of Meals: 6

Required Material:

- Carrots, which peeled and sliced 2 pounds' worth. Exactly one spoonful of pure, unfiltered olive oil
- Peel and finely chop 1 medium onion
- 4 medium potatoes, cleaned and diced. Three peeled and minced cloves of garlic. Vegetable Stock, 6 Cups
- A dash of pepper, a dash of salt, and a dash of fresh thyme, all totaling 1 teaspoon

Step-By-Step Procedure:

1. Heat the oil for 30 seconds in a big saucepan. Toss in the chopped vegetables and minced garlic and onions. Cook the veggies for 10 mins on medium heat.
2. It's time to incorporate the stock and crank up the stove to medium-high.
3. After the soup has come to a boil, reduce the heat and boil for another 50-60 mins.
4. Use an immersion blender or a conventional blender to puree the soup until smooth, taking care not to burn

yourself. Return the soup to the pan if you blended it.

5. The salt, pepper, and thyme should be added now. Keep cooking at a medium temperature for another 15 minutes. Provide sizzling

Dietary Composition: Caloric Intake: 80, Quantity of fat: 4g, Quantity of Carbohydrates: 11g, Quantity of Protein: 2g, Quantity of Fiber: 3g

49. Chicken and Lemon Soup

Readiness Time: 15-17 minutes Time needed to cook: 10 minutes Quantity of Meals: 4

Required Material:

- Long-grain white rice: Half cup of
- A carrot
- Low-sodium chicken broth: 2 cans (14 ½ ounces)
- Chicken breasts, cooked and diced: Two mugs
- Garlic: 1 clove
- Freshly squeezed lemon juice: 1/4 cup
- Red sweet pepper: 1/2 cup
- Cornstarch: 1 tablespoon
- Evaporated milk without fat: 1 can (12 ounces)
- Basil, just cut: 2 tablespoons

Step-By-Step Procedure:

1. Place the broth in a medium-sized pot and bring to a boil.
2. Cook the rice for Ten mins, or until it is cooked, after adding the garlic, lemon juice, bell pepper, and chicken.
3. In a small dish, whisk together cornstarch and 1 tbsp of the evaporated milk; then, while whisking, add the cornstarch mixture to the soup.
4. Bring the ingredients to a low boil, then turn off the heat and serve the soup with a sprinkle of basil.

Dietary Composition: Caloric Intake: 125, Quantity of fat: 2.5g, Quantity of Carbohydrates: 10g, Quantity of Protein: 13g, Quantity of Fiber: 1g

50. Chicken Raisin Stew

Readiness Time: 20-23 minutes Time needed to cook: 55 minutes Quantity of Meals: 8

Required Material:

- Deboned chicken for stew: 3 pounds
- Salt: 1/2 teaspoon
- Black pepper, freshly ground: 1/4 teaspoon
- Turmeric Powder: One Tablespoon
- Saffron: 1/2 teaspoon
- A onion
- Chopped fresh Italian parsley: three teaspoons' worth
- Raisin: one cup
- Orange juice: One cup
- Ginger: Two tsp
- Water: one mug
- Cinnamon and cornstarch: 1 teaspoon each
- Cooked brown, wild, or white rice: Four cups

Step-By-Step Procedure:

1. To thoroughly clean the chicken, place it in the sink.
2. Transfer to a large saucepan, such as a Dutch oven.
3. The chicken, together with the salt, pepper, turmeric, saffron, onion, and parsley, should be heated in a covered stockpot.
4. In the meanwhile, in a small saucepan, stir together cornstarch, ginger, cinnamon, orange juice, and raisins.
5. For a thicker consistency, cook the raisins over low heat for approximately 10 minutes, stirring regularly.
6. Take caution while pouring the raisin mixture into the blender, but once you do, blend it until it's completely smooth.

Covering the chicken with the raisin purée and baking it.

7. For a flavorful sauce and tender chicken, simmer all the ingredients together for 45 minutes.
8. Serve by spooning some rice into 8 (or 6 or 4) bowls, topping it with a piece or two of chicken, and then topping that with some stew.

Dietary Composition: Caloric Intake: 310, Quantity of fat: 7g, Quantity of Carbohydrates: 32g, Quantity of Protein: 22g, Quantity of Fiber: 4g

51. <u>Chickpea and Lentil Bean Soup</u>

Readiness Time: 25-27 minutes Time needed to cook: 1 hour Quantity of Meals: 4

Required Material:

- EVO oil: 2 TBSP
- Big celery stalks chopped: 4
- Minced garlic cloves and Onion: 2 of each
- Rinsed lentils: 1 cup
- Water: Liters 1,40
- Cinnamon, Ginger: 1/2 teaspoons (each)
- Turmeric: 3/4 teaspoon
- Cumin: 1 tsp.
- Rinsed chickpeas: 16 ounces
- Diced tomatoes, three medium-sized
- A lemon: Half only juice + another half finely sliced
- Minced fresh herbs like cilantro or parsley: 1/2 mug

Step-By-Step Procedure:

1. Start sauté the onions in EVO oil.
2. After three minutes, put the garlic and celery and keep cooking until the onions are golden brown.
3. Lentils, water, and spices are combined; the mixture is brought to a boil before being reduced to a simmer for forty minutes.

4. Simmer for 15 minutes after adding the chickpeas and tomatoes as well as any additional water and seasonings.
5. When ready to serve, divide the soup into dishes and top with fresh lemon juice and some cilantro or parsley.
6. Serve immediately with a slice or two of lemon on the side.

Dietary Composition: Caloric Intake 360, Quantity of fat: 8g, Quantity of Carbohydrates: 58g, Quantity of Protein: 15g, Quantity of Fiber: 11g

52. <u>Chickpea Soup</u>

Readiness Time: 15-18 minutes Time needed to cook: 25 minutes Quantity of Meals: 4

Required Material:

- Olive oil: 1-quarter cup
- Garlic: 4
- Onions: one cup
- Chickpeas: (15-ounce) Two cans
- Lemon juice: 1-quarter cup
- Parsley: 1/2 mug
- Bay leaf: 1 sea
- Salt: 1+1/2 teaspoons
- Moroccan spice oil
- Water: Four mugs

Step-By-Step Procedure:

1. Heat oil. Cook garlic and onion for 10 minutes, tossing periodically, until they brown.

2. Stir chickpeas, parsley, and a bay leaf into 4 cups of water, cover, and bring to a low boil.
3. Season with salt and dried bay leaf after 15 minutes of lidded simmering.
4. Blend the soup in stages in a food processor until smooth.
5. After pureeing, add lemon juice and return soup to the pan.
6. Add Moroccan olive oil and parsley over the soup and serve.

Dietary Composition: Caloric Intake 150, Quantity of fat: 3.5g, Quantity of Carbohydrates: 22g, Quantity of Fiber: 5g, Quantity of Protein: 8g

53. Cold Cucumber Soup

Readiness Time: 10-13 minutes Time needed to cook: 0 minutes Quantity of Meals: 4-6

Required Material:

- Citrus juice
- Parsley, fresh, chopped: 1/2 cup
- Cucumbers, medium: Two
- Chicken broth: One half cup
- Fat-free plain yogurt: one cup
- Prepare to taste with salt and freshly ground black pepper
- Fat-free half-and-half: One 1/2 cup
- Finely diced fresh dill

Step-By-Step Procedure:

1. Combine the cucumbers, parsley, and lemon juice in a blender or food processor and pulse until smooth.
2. Put half of the puree on a platter and put the other half aside.
3. Blend the yogurt, cream, and broth together in a medium bowl.
4. Blend the ingredients as usual, but this time add half of the yogurt mixture and blend again until smooth.
5. After adding salt and pepper, store in the fridge in an airtight container.
6. The leftover yogurt mixture and the purée should go through the same process again.

7. Sprinkle in some fresh dill before serving, and give the soup a thorough stir.

Dietary Composition: Caloric Intake: 100, Quantity of fat: 0g, Quantity of Carbohydrates: 18g, Quantity of Protein: 3g, Quantity of Fiber: 1g

54. Greek Gazpacho

Readiness Time: 20-23 minutes Time needed to cook: 3 hours Quantity of Meals: 4

Required Material:

- White bread, stale: two slices
- Oregano, dry: one tablespoon
- Crushed garlic cloves: Three to four peeled
- Bunch of fresh parsley: 2 tbsp.
- The Red Wine Vinegar and Oil of olive use the same quantity: 1/4 Cups
- Roasted red pepper: one big
- Big green sweet pepper, roasted: 1
- Onions: Two (red)
- Big English cucumber, diced: 1
- Roughly sliced ripe tomatoes: 4
- Sun-dried black olives: 3/4 cup
- A pinch of black pepper
- Feta cheese cubes: 1 mug
- Olive oil ice cubes: about 4-6

Step-By-Step Procedure:

1. To make a wet paste, combine the bread with olive oil, garlic, and parsley in a food processor.
2. The oil and vinegar should be pulsed in until they are evenly distributed.
3. Get out a big bowl and dump the contents of the processor in it. Get it aside.
4. Throw in peppers, onions, cucumber, tomatoes, and olives into your food processor.
5. Pulse the blender to get a coarser chop. Mix the saved bread-garlic combination with the vegetable cocktail and the pepper.
6. Wrap in plastic and place in the fridge for at least three hours.

7. Using feta and olive oil ice cubes as a garnish, serve cold.

Dietary Composition: Caloric Intake 80, Quantity of fat: 1.5g, Quantity of Carbohydrates: 14g, Quantity of Protein: 2g, Quantity of Fiber: 2g

55. Italian Bean Soup

Readiness Time: 17 minutes Time needed to cook:23 minutes Quantity of Meals: 4

Required Material:

- EVO oil: one tbsp
- Use the same quantity of Onion, garlic, stalk celery: 1
- White kidney beans: Two cans
- Chicken broth: 1 can;
- Pepper: One-fourth of a teaspoon
- Water: 2mugs
- Sprig of thyme dry: one pinch
- Fresh, finely cut spinach: 1 Bunch
- Juice from a freshly squeezed lemon: one tablespoon
- Grated Parmesan cheese, for topping

Step-By-Step Procedure:

1. Before adding the onion and celery, heat the oil. After 30 more seconds, add garlic.
2. Boil the beans, broth, two cups of water, pepper, and thyme in a big pot. Boil for 15 mins.
3. Blend the soup after reserving 2 cups of the same. Return it to the pot with the saved beans and heat.
4. Boil, add spinach, and cook until wilted. Whisk in lemon juice after removing from heat.
5. Before serving, sprinkle grated Parmesan over the four portions.

Dietary Composition: Caloric Intake 220, Quantity of fat: 5g, Quantity of Carbohydrates: 33g, Quantity of Protein: 11g, Quantity of Fiber: 7g

56. Kakavia (Fish Soup)

Readiness Time: 20-23 minutes Time needed to cook: 50 minutes Quantity of Meals: 6

Required Material:

- Vegetables used in the same proportion: (onions, stalk celery, potatoes, carrots): Two pieces of each
- Marjoram: 1 tablespoon dried
- Salt and pepper
- Fresh cod, cut into pieces: 2 pounds
- Parsley: 1/4 cup
- Fresh grey mullet, deboned: 2 pounds
- EVO oil: 1/2 cup
- Juice of a lemon
- Mussels, cleaned and bearded: 1 pound

Step-By-Step Procedure:

1. Boil 6 pints of water in a large pot. Cover and simmer chopped vegetables, marjoram, salt, and pepper for 30 minutes.
2. Clean seafood correctly. After 30 minutes, add the fish, mushrooms, and parsley to the boiling water for 20 more minutes.
3. Take away the fish and mussels from the pot using a slotted spoon and place on a dish.
4. Strain the stock, pushing the softer vegetables through the strainer with a wooden spoon. Return the filtered stock

to the pan and add the olive oil and lemon juice.

5. Boil, then cook slowly maximum 5 mins.
6. Serve warm

Dietary Composition: Caloric Intake 210, Quantity of fat: 8 g, Quantity of Carbohydrates: 6g, Quantity of Fiber: 0g, Quantity of Protein: 26g

57. <u>Leeky Parsley Soup</u>

Readiness Time: 13 minutes Time needed to cook: 15 minutes Quantity of Meals: 4-6

Required Material:

- Oil: 1 tbsp.
- Bunch fresh flat-leaf parsley + parsley leaves reserved for garnishing: 1
- Leeks: 3
- Low-sodium vegetable or chicken broth or water: 4 cups
- Green onions: Fuor
- Unpeeled zucchini: one
- Salt: 2 tsp.

Step-By-Step Procedure:

1. Apply the oil to a big stockpot, then warm.
2. Stirring often, cook the leeks and parsley in the oil for approximately 5 minutes, or until the leeks have lost their vibrant green color and become translucent.
3. Cook the onions and zucchini in a pot of boiling stock or water, for about 10 mins.
4. When is ready, cooling the soup for ten minutes.
5. Sprinkle with chopped parsley and serve immediately.

Dietary Composition: Caloric Intake 116, Quantity of fat: 0.9g, Quantity of Carbohydrates: 20.2g, Quantity of Protein: 4.4g, Quantity of Fiber: 3.9g

58. <u>Lemony Soup</u>

Readiness Time: 10-14 minutes Time needed to cook: 25 minutes Quantity of Meals: 8

Required Material:

- Low-sodium chicken or veggie stock: 8 cups
- Flour: 1/4 cup
- High-quality olive oil: Two Tbsp
- A stick of butter: about 2 tbsp
- Orzo: 1 Cup
- Eggs: Four
- Squeezed lemon juice: 3/4 cups
- To taste, season with sea salt and a pinch of white pepper
- Slices of lemon: 8

Step-By-Step Procedure:

1. In a soup pot, boil stock.
2. Unite oil, flour, and butter in a small bowl. Slowly mix in two cups of boiling stock. Slowly whisk the flour mixture into the pot and simmer for 10 mins. Add the orzo after 5 minutes and stir often.
3. Whisk the lemon juice and eggs in a separate bowl until frothy. Slowly whisk the egg mixture.
4. Combine the eggs and soup. Simmering soup should thicken after 10 minutes.
5. Serve the soup with salt and pepper. Serve with lemon slices.

Dietary Composition: Caloric Intake 35, Quantity of fat: 0g, Quantity of Carbohydrates: 7g, Quantity of Protein: 0g, Quantity of Fiber: 0g

59. <u>Lentil Soup</u>

Readiness Time: 14 minutes Time needed to cook: 50-60 minutes Quantity of Meals: 8

Required Material:

- Rinsed lentils: enough for 2 cups
- Pure olive oil: about 120ml

- Onions, medium: 2
- Big carrot: 1
- A single big red pepper
- Tomato sauce: A third of a cup
- Bay leaves: Three
- Sweet paprika: one Tbsp
- Garlic: total 8 cloves (3 crushed; 5 minced)
- Oregano: 2 tablespoons
- Salt: 2 1/2 teaspoons
- Red wine vinegar: 1/4 cup
- Water: Eight mugs + a little for cooking lentils

Step-By-Step Procedure:

1. Put the lentils and some water in a big saucepan and cook them. Simmer the water for a minute after bringing it to a boil. The lentils need to be drained.
2. Get out a pot and fill it with oil, onions, carrots, peppers, bay leaves, tomato sauce, paprika, and crushed garlic. Reintroduce the lentils. After adding 8 cups of water, bring the soup to a boil.
3. Cover it. Lentils should be cooked for 50-60 minutes, or until they are tender. Pick up the bay leaves and throw them out with the trash. Add the vinegar, salt, oregano, and garlic that has been minced. Cook for two minutes longer. Provide warm.

Dietary Composition: Caloric Intake 230, Quantity of fat: 2.5g, Quantity of Carbohydrates: 32g, Quantity of Protein: 14g, Quantity of Fiber: 10g

60. **Mediterranean Red Lentil Bean Soup**

Readiness Time: 2 hours' Time needed to cook: 30-40 minutes Quantity of Meals: 4-6

Required Material:

- Chicken stock: 8 cups.
- Tomatoes, diced: 2
- Onions: Two
- Cumin powder: 1 teaspoon
- High-quality olive oil: Two tablespoons

- Potato: Half
- Cleaned Spinach and lentils beans: 2 cups of each
- Spices and salt
- Carrots: 2

Step-By-Step Procedure:

1. The water that the lentils were soaked in should be discarded once they have been drained.
2. The amount and kind of lentils you choose will determine how long you need to heat them until they are tender. A lentil may be used as a cooking time indicator.
3. Over moderate heat, add the olive oil to the soup pot. You may use it to sauté some onions and carrots. The stock, tomatoes, spinach, and potato should be placed in a saucepan and brought to a simmer. Spice it up to your liking.
4. Lentils should be cooked for 30–40 minutes, but you should check on them often. It may be necessary to add more water and olive oil. Serve

Dietary Composition: Caloric Intake 238, Quantity of fat: 4.3g, Quantity of Carbohydrates: 36.2g, Quantity of Protein: 12.3g, Quantity of Fiber: 9.6g

61. **Minestrone Soup**

Readiness Time: 20-23 minutes Time needed to cook: 8 hours and 30 minutes Quantity of Meals: 6

Required Material:

- Onion, diced: One
- Chopped tomatoes: one (28-ounce) can
- Navy beans: two (14.5 ounces) cans
- Celery stalks: 3
- Chicken stock: 4 cups
- Carrots: Three
- Chicken sausage links Italian: Four
- Orzo: 1 mug
- Zucchinis: 3
- Parmesan for serving: a half cup

- Bay leaves: two
- Sprigs of thyme: 2
- Dried sage: half tsp

Step-By-Step Procedure:

1. Cook for 8hrs using a 5-quart slow cooker the components present on the list, except orzo and zucchini.
2. They should be added during the last 30 minutes of cooking time.
3. Sprinkle the soup with salt and serve it in 8 dishes, topping each with a bay leaf and a spoonful of Parmesan cheese.

Dietary Composition: Caloric Intake 208, Quantity of fat: 5.1g, Quantity of Carbohydrates: 30.7g, Quantity of Protein: 8.9g, Quantity of Fiber: 3.9g

62. Moroccan Vegetable Stew

Readiness Time: 15-30 minutes Time needed to cook: 30 minutes Quantity of Meals: 8

Required Material:

- Cut into 1-inch cubes without peeling medium eggplant: ONE
- Ocean salt: one tbsp
- Little onions: 6
- Minced garlic: Amount: 4
- EVO oil: 2 tbsp
- Cinnamon powder: enough for 1 1/2 teaspoons
- Spices (ground turmeric, cloves): 1 teaspoon of each
- Cumin: one tsp
- Spot of red pepper pieces
- Flavorful black pepper that has just been ground
- Picked tomatoes (strip them anyway you want): Three
- Zucchinis: 3
- Medium yams: 2
- Celery stalks: three
- Green chile pepper: 1

- chickpeas, drained and rinsed: One 15-ounce can of
- Red kidney beans, after cooking: one 15-ounce can
- Natural chicken stock: 1 cup
- Parsley, Italian, Minced: 2 Tablespoons (level leaf)

Step-By-Step Procedure:

1. The eggplants should be placed in a colander and seasoned with salt. Cover with a paper towel and place one plate on top of them. To make it easier to extract the eggplant liquids for this recipe, arrange the cans of beans on top of the dish. Wait 15-30 minutes.
2. Meanwhile, heat a large skillet or Dutch oven. Saute the onions and garlic in 1 tablespoon of oil for just 5 minutes. Add more oil and then the aubergines; they will be ready when they get a golden colour.
3. Incorporate cinnamon, cumin, turmeric, cloves, cayenne and dark pepper. Blend for two minutes of time. Put everything else (except the parsley) in a Dutch oven.
4. Bring to a boil, then turn the heat down to low, cover and simmer the vegetables for 20 minutes. Add the parsley, then serve with pita on the side.

Dietary Composition: Caloric Intake: 190, Quantity of fat: 7g, Quantity of Carbohydrates: 28g, Quantity of Protein: 5g, Quantity of Fiber: 6g

63. Pumpkin Soup

Readiness Time: 15-17 minutes Time needed to cook: 50 minutes Quantity of Meals: 6

Required Material:

- Butter, unsalted: 1/4 cup
- Onion: one
- Ginger, grated: 2 tablespoons
- Garlic: 2
- Vegetable stock: 8 cups
- Pumpkin: 3 cups

- Parsley: 3 tbsp
- Finely chopped fresh chives: One-fourth cup
- Salt: two teaspoons
- Powdered pepper: half tsp
- Nutmeg: one-eighth teaspoon

Step-By-Step Procedure:

1. In a big saucepan, loosen the butter. Prepare the dish by adding the onion, garlic, and ginger. Cook slowly the onions for approximately 5 minutes.
2. Combine the pumpkin, stock, and parsley in a pot. The soup should be brought to a boil. Cover the saucepan, reduce the flame, and cook for 40 to 45 mins. Add some pepper, salt, and nutmeg to taste.
3. Stir in the chives after you've carefully pureed the soup using an immersion blender or a conventional blender to get a silky texture...

Dietary Composition: Caloric Intake 130, Quantity of fat: 4g, Quantity of Carbohydrates: 21g, Quantity of Protein: 4g, Quantity of Fiber: 4g

64. Roasted Yellow Bell Pepper Soup

Readiness Time: 15-18 minutes Time needed to cook: 30 minutes Quantity of Meals: 6

Required Material:

- A Leek, white portion only, peeled, trimmed, washed, split in half lengthwise, and sliced thinly.
- A carrot,
- Evo oil: 1/4 cup
- Medium Yukon gold potatoes: 2
- Sweet paprika and thyme: one teaspoon of each
- Half a stalk of celery with the ends removed
- Garlic: 4
- Salt: one and a half teaspoons
- Basil leaf: Half a cup
- Pepper: half a teaspoon

- Big yellow peppers: 4
- Heavy cream: half a cup
- Small hot banana pepper: one
- Stock (either vegetable, chicken, or turkey): Four cups
- Shredded cheese of the Gruyere or Swiss kind: 1/2 cup

Step-By-Step Procedure:

1. Warm oil for 30 seconds in a large pot. Mix garlic, leeks, carrots, and celery. Adjust with salt and pepper. Leeks should be soft after 10 minutes.
2. Potatoes, paprika, and thyme, Two minutes in a medium pan. Add chicken stock and roasted peppers. Medium heat should boil the soup. Reduce heat and cook for 20 minutes.
3. Incorporate basil. Blend the soup in a standard or immersion blender until smooth. Cream, cheese, and remaining salt and pepper must add. The soup is ready when the cheese has melted and it is smooth. Provide sizzling

Dietary Composition: Caloric Intake 50, Quantity of fat: 0g, Quantity of Carbohydrates: 11g, Quantity of Protein: 1g, Quantity of Fiber: 2g

65. Spicy Lentil and Spinach Soup

Readiness Time: 10-13 minutes Time needed to cook: 30 minutes Quantity of Meals: 4 -6

Required Material:

- EVO oil: two tbsp
- Onion and garlic: 1 of each
- Mint flakes: 2 teaspoons
- Spices in the same proportion (sumac, cumin, Coriander, red peppers): 1½ tsp.
- Sea salt
- Black pepper
- Pinch of sugar
- Flour: 1 tbsp.
- Water: 3 cups, more if needed
- Low-sodium vegetable broth: 6 cups

- Brown lentils: 1½ cups
- Frozen cut leaf spinach (no need to thaw): 10-12 oz.
- Parsley: 2 cups
- Lime juice: 2 tbsp.

Step-By-Step Procedure:

1. Sauté chopped onions in 2 tablespoons of olive oil in a large ceramic saucepan for 4 minutes. With garlic, dried mint, spices, sugar, and flour, cook for 2 minutes, stirring often.
2. Slowly cook the lentils and spinach for 5 minutes after the water and broth boil.
3. After 20 minutes, covered, the lentils are ready. Remove from heat and toss in chopped parsley and lime juice. Serve hot pita or rustic Italian bread together. Resting ingredients for five minutes improves the flavor.

Dietary Composition: Caloric Intake 250, Quantity of fat: 5g, Quantity of Carbohydrates: 42g, Quantity of Protein: 12g, Quantity of Fiber: 8g

66. Tuscan White Bean Stew

Readiness Time: 20-23 minutes Time needed to cook: 1 hour and 15 minutes Quantity of Meals: 4

Required Material:

- A cut of entire grain bread (cut into 1/2-inch blocks)
- Cannellini beans (flushed, doused for the time being, and depleted): two mugs
- Cloves of smashed garlic: 6 + 2 quartered
- Slashed new rosemary: 1 tablespoon + 6 twigs
- EVO oil: Three tbsp
- Carrots: 3
- Inlet leaf: just one
- Vegetable stock: 1/2 cup
- A slashed yellow onion
- Water: 6 cups
- A teaspoon of salt
- Dark pepper: a quarter tsp

Step-By-Step Procedure:

1. To prepare bread garnishes, heat oil in a skillet and sauté 2 cloves of quartered garlic for 1 minute. To flavour your oil with garlic, remove the jar from the heat. Discard garlic pieces.
2. Heat again. Add bread blocks and gently sauté for 3–5 minutes, mixing. Set it away in a small basin.
3. Bring white beans, sound leaf, water, and 1/2 teaspoon salt to a boil in the soup pot.
4. Cover and cook beans for 60–75 minutes. Save 1/2 cup cooking fluid from cannellini beans. Remove leaf. Put the cooked beans in the bowl and save for later.
5. Mix 1/2 cup cooked beans and cooking fluid in the small basin. Crush with a fork to make glue.
6. Heat the pot and add olive oil. Sauté carrots and onion till tender and fresh after 6–7 minutes.
7. Cook garlic until relaxed. It will take a minute. Add the bean mixture, pepper, rosemary, and vegetable stock. Heat to boiling, then lower the flame and stew slowly. Wait 5 minutes.
8. Place the stew in warmed dishes and serve with bread; garnish each dish with a rosemary twig. Serve.

Dietary Composition: Caloric Intake 331, Quantity of fat: 6.4g, Quantity of Protein: 12.4g, Quantity of Carbohydrates: 51.4g, Quantity of Fiber: 9.2g

67. Veggie Barley Soup

Readiness Time: 20-23 minutes Time needed to cook: 1 hour and 30 minutes Quantity of Meals: 4

Required Material:

- Stalks of celery: Two
- Big carrots: 2
- Vegetable broth: two quarts
- Barley: for one cup
- Garbanzo beans: 1 15-ounce can
- Zucchini, diced: 1

- Diced tomatoes: one (14.5 ounce) can
- Onion, chopped: 1
- Bay leaves: 3
- Parsley, sugar, garlic in powder, Worcestershire sauce: use 1 tsp of each
- Curry Powder: One Tablespoon
- Black pepper, ground: 1/2 teaspoon
- A pinch of salt

Step-By-Step Procedure:

1. Warm the stock in a large soup pot.
2. Unite together celery, carrots, barley, garbanzo beans, zucchini, tomatoes, onion, bay leaves, parsley, sugar, garlic powder, Worcestershire sauce, paprika, curry powder, sea salt, and pepper.
3. Slowly boil the mixture, cover, and lower the heat.
4. Cook the soup for 90 minutes or until desired consistency.
5. Remove bay leaves and serve immediately.

Dietary Composition: Caloric Intake 158, Quantity of fat: 2.3g, Quantity of Carbohydrates: 28.2g, Quantity of Protein: 5.3g, Quantity of Fiber: 7.3g

POULTRY

68. Bacon-Wrapped Quail

Readiness Time: 6 hours' Time needed to cook: 20 minutes Quantity of Meals: 4

Required Material:

- Whole quail, rinsed and dried: 4 (7-ounce)
- Oil, divided: 1/2 cup (EVO)
- Garlic: 3 or 4
- Lemon: zest Half tsp +juice 2 Tbsp
- Grated orange zest: one tbsp
- Sweet paprika: 1 tsp
- Cinnamon: 1/2 teaspoon
- Thyme: 2 teaspoons
- A pinch salt and pepper
- Strips bacon: 8
- A large lemon, cut into wedges

Step-By-Step Procedure:

1. In a big baking dish, combine the oil, garlic, zest, and juice from all the citrus fruits, paprika, cinnamon, thyme, salt, and pepper.
2. Combine everything in a bowl and drizzle with marinade and olive oil. Refrigerate the bowl, uncovered, for at least six hours.
3. Let's hope the temperature in here goes up.
4. Tie the legs of the quail together with butcher's twine and tuck the tips of the wings back under the birds for a uniform roast.
5. Turn on the oven and set the temperature to 400 F. Wrap each quail in bacon and tuck the ends underneath it.
6. For one minute, heat the residual oil in a big cast-iron pan.
7. Place the quail inside and let them to cook free for 20 minutes
8. When ready hold off for 5 minutes and serve with lemon wedges.

Dietary Composition: Caloric Intake 340, Quantity of fat: 14g, Carbohydrate: 0g, Quantity of Fiber: 0g, Quantity of Protein: 37g

69. Chicken Breasts with Spinach and Feta

Readiness Time: 15-17 minutes Time needed to cook: 35 minutes Quantity of Meals: 4

Required Material:

- Fresh spinach: half cup
- Chives and dill: a total 8 tablespoons (the half of each)
- Feta cheese: 1/2 cup crumbled
- Ricotta: 1/3 cup
- Chicken breasts: four
- Salt: one plus half tsp
- Pepper and sweet paprika: each 1/2 teaspoon
- EVO oil: 2 tablespoons
- Dry white wine: haf cup
- Red onions: 2 tablespoons
- A clove garlic, peeled and smashed
- all-purpose flour: 2 tablespoons

- Chicken or turkey stock: 1 cup
- Unsalted butter: Two tbsp
- Heavy cream: 1/3 cup

Step-By-Step Procedure:

1. Mix the feta and ricotta with the spinach and chives in a medium bowl. Reserve.
2. Create a 3-inch-long cut in the thickest section of the chicken breast with a sharp knife. For the pocket to develop correctly, the incision has to be made approximately two-thirds of the way through the chicken breast.
3. Fill the pocket with 25% spinach cheese. Toothpicks secure the door. Cook the chicken twice more. Salt, pepper, and paprika on the chicken before cooking.
4. Loose butter and oil in a big pan. Chicken should be roasted for 3–4 mins. per side. Heat the chicken before adding wine.
5. Serve 2 minutes after the wine has almost disappeared. Add onions, garlic, and flour. Two minutes.
6. Add stock and cook the sauce, now add the chicken. Covered skillets take 25 minutes.
7. Simmer until thick after adding cream. Salt & pepper to taste immediately.
8. Slice the chicken into bite-sized pieces. Sauce on the chicken and eat!

Dietary Composition: Caloric Intake: 370, Quantity of fat: 18g, Quantity of Carbohydrates: 5g, Quantity of Protein: 44 Quantity of Sodium: 690m Quantity of Fiber: 2g

70. Chicken Livers in Red Wine

Readiness Time: 10-13 minutes Time needed to cook: 10-15 minutes Quantity of Meals: 4

Required Material:

- Liver from one bird: (1 lb.)
- Chicken broth with butter: 1 cup and half
- One small onion
- Flour, generic: one tbsp
- Fresh parsley: two tbsp

- Red wine: half cup
- Salt & pepper

Step-By-Step Procedure:

1. Chicken livers should be well cleaned and drained before use. After bringing the broth to a boil in a small saucepan, reduce the heat and let it to simmer.
2. Butter should be melted in a separate pan. Sauté the onion in a little bit of olive oil until soft, then add the chicken livers and cook for 3 to 5 minutes on high heat, turning often to avoid scorching.
3. Flour the livers and sprinkle butter, put in the pan, then cook till a sauce develops. Always be stirring to avoid clumping.
4. Slowly add the wine and bring to a simmer over high heat, stirring occasionally, for several minutes. Stirring frequently, gradually pour the heated broth into the pan holding the livers.
5. Reduce heat and continue simmering, uncovered, for 5-10 minutes to thicken sauce. Season to taste with salt and pepper.
6. Garnish with chopped parsley and serve immediately accompanied with mashed potatoes.

Dietary Composition: Caloric Intake 143, Quantity of fat: 5.4g, Quantity of Carbohydrates: 1.1g, Quantity of Protein: 20.4g, Quantity of Fiber: 0g

71. Chicken Salad: Pine Nuts, Raisins, Fennel

Readiness Time: 1-hour Time needed to cook: 0 minutes Serve: 1 large bowe

Required Material:

For the dressing:

- (Extra-virgin) olive-oil: 1 tbsp
- Mayonnaise: 3 tbsp.
- Small clove garlic mashed with sea salt: Half

- A Pinch cayenne
- Squeezed lemon juice: 1 tbsp.

For the salad:

- Onion: 3 tbsp
- Fennel: ⅓ cup
- Already cooked chicken: one mug
- Golden raisins, pine nuts (toasted), parsley (flat-leaf): used of each 2 tbsp
- Sea salt
- Freshly ground pepper

Step-By-Step Procedure:

1. In a small bowl, combine the EVO oil, mayonnaise, garlic, cayenne pepper, lemon juice, and salt & pepper to taste.
2. In a separate dish, mix the onion, fennel, chicken, raisins, pine nuts, and parsley.
3. Then, add the dressing and whisk gently to combine.
4. Put in the fridge for at least an hour after seasoning with salt and pepper so the flavors may develop.

Dietary Composition: Caloric Intake 370, Quantity of fat: 15g, Quantity of Protein: 22g, Quantity of Carbohydrates: 36g, Quantity of Fiber: 6g

72. Chicken Tagine with Lemons and Olives

Readiness Time: 23-25 minutes Time needed to cook: 45-50 minutes Quantity of Meals: 4

Required Material:

- Finely minced garlic cloves: three
- Preserved lemons: 1.2 teaspoons
- Minced fresh ginger: 1 tablespoon
- Onions: total 4 (Two should be chopped, while the other two should be sliced.
- Sweet paprika, 1 tbsp
- Fresh cilantro: One cup
- Fresh parsley: two tablespoons
- Cumin: half a teaspoon

- Salt: 2 tsp
- Saffron threads: about a quarter of a teaspoon, and half a cup of simmering water
- Pure olive oil: A quarter cup
- Bay Leaves: three
- Potatoes: 2 big
- Chicken legs and thighs: 4
- Tomatoes, ripe: 2
- Green olives, half mug
- Water: a cup's worth

Step-By-Step Procedure:

1. The following ingredients are placed in a food processor: garlic, ginger, half of a preserved lemon, chopped onions, chickpeas, paprika, cumin, a teaspoon of salt, a couple of tablespoons of cilantro, parsley, saffron soaked in water, olive oil, and bouillon cubes. Make sure everything is cut up and mixed in properly.
2. Combine half of the marinade with the chicken in a large bowl. Marinate the chicken by tossing it in the sauce. Season the chicken with the remaining salt.
3. Throw the remaining basil, chopped tomatoes, potatoes, and sliced onions into the Dutch oven.
4. Toss the veggies in the marinade so that they are all evenly coated. Combine the veggies with the water and stir.
5. The chicken should be placed on the veggies. The chicken is topped with sliced tomatoes, olives, and one cup of cilantro. Cut the remaining lemon into six wedges and add them.
6. Keep the tagine covered and simmer it over low heat. Set the timer for 45 to 50 minutes.
7. Don't open the lid or stir the tagine while it's cooking.
8. Remove the bay leaves and arrange the tangine on the table, food in the middle.

Dietary Composition: Caloric Intake 330, Quantity of fat: 17g, Quantity of Carbohydrates: 13g, Quantity of Protein: 30g, Quantity of Fiber: 4g

73. Chicken with Roasted Vegetables

Readiness Time: 18-20 minutes Time needed to cook: 40 minutes Serve 2

Required Material:

- Large zucchini, diagonally sliced: one
- Baby new potatoes: 250g
- Firm plum tomatoes: 6
- A Red onion
- Yellow pepper: one
- Already pitted black olives: 12
- Chicken breast fillets: two
- Green pesto: 1 rounded tbsp.
- (Extra-virgin-olive) oil: 3 tbsp.

Step-By-Step Procedure:

1. Bake at 400F for 10 minutes. Using a roasting pan, arrange vegetables such as zucchini, potatoes, tomatoes, onions, and peppers.
2. Sprinkle some salt and pepper on the chicken breasts before placing them on top of the veggies.
3. In a small bowl, combine the pesto and extra-virgin olive oil. Rub the mixture all over the chicken. After 10 minutes, take the cover off and put the pan back on the burner to finish cooking the chicken.

Dietary Composition: Caloric Intake 545, Quantity of fat: 22.2g, Quantity of Carbohydrates: 40.3g, Quantity of Protein: 43.2g, Quantity of Fiber: 6.5g

74. Coconut Chicken

Readiness Time: 15-17 minutes Time needed to cook: 10 minutes Serve 4

Required Material:

- Coconut: 20g
- Coconut oil: 7.5 mL
- Almond flour: 30g
- Egg: 1

- Chicken breast: 100g
- Sea salt

Step-By-Step Procedure:

1. Shredded the coconut and combine it in a dish with the ground almonds and the salt.
2. Coat the chicken thoroughly with the flour mixture, then dip it in the beaten egg, and then roll it in the flour mixture.
3. Golden brown the chicken's crust by frying it in a skillet brushed with coconut oil over medium heat.
4. Bake the chicken for approximately 10 minutes at 350 degrees Fahrenheit.

Dietary Composition: Caloric Intake 663, Quantity of fat: 41g, Quantity of Carbohydrates: 42g, Quantity of Protein: 26g, Quantity of Fiber: 5g

75. Delicious Mediterranean Chicken

Readiness Time: 20-23 minutes Time needed to cook: 25 minutes Serve 6

Required Material:

- Extra-virgin olive oil: 2 tsp.
- White wine: 1/2 cup
- Chicken breasts: six
- Minced garlic cloves: 3
- Salt and pepper: 2 teaspoons
- Onion: 1/2 cup
- Tomatoes: 3 cups
- Kalamata olives: 1/2 cup
- Fresh parsley: 1/4 cup
- Thyme: two tsp
- Salt from the sea.

Step-By-Step Procedure:

1. Put the oil and three teaspoons of white wine in a skillet and heat it.
2. If you want golden chicken, cook it for around 6 minutes on each side. Remove the chicken and place it on a serving dish.
3. Before adding the tomatoes, sauté the garlic and onions for about three minutes.

4. After 5 minutes, reduce the heat and simmer for another 10 mins. Then, after 5 more minutes of simmering, add the thyme.
5. The chicken should be cooked to an internal temperature of 165 degrees Fahrenheit, which may be achieved via slow cooking. After including the olives and parsley, cook for an additional minute. Add salt and pepper, and it's ready to be served.

Dietary Composition: Caloric Intake 350, Quantity of fat: 16g, Quantity of Carbohydrates: 18g, Quantity of Protein: 33g, Quantity of Fiber: 2g

76. **Goose Braised with Citrus**

Readiness Time: 15-17 minutes Time needed to cook: 3-4 hours Quantity of Meals: 6

Required Material:

- Onion: 2
- Carrot: 1
- Stalk celery
- Grapefruit
- Oranges: 2
- A lemon and 1 lime
- Olive oil: A tablespoon
- Goose: 3-pound
- Port wine: 1/2 cup
- Honey: 1/4 cup
- Red wine: 2 cups

Step-By-Step Procedure:

1. The oven has to be preheated to 350 degrees F.
2. The carrot should be peeled and sliced into quarters. Slice the onions into thin strips. Grapefruits, oranges, lemons, and limes should all be peeled and cut into quarters.
3. Put the oil in a large Dutch oven and heat it over medium heat. Get both sides of the geese nice and toasty.
4. The fruit and veggies need to be cooked for 5 minutes with steady stirring. Put the wine in the container, divide it in half, add the honey, and store it in the fridge.
5. After the liquid comes to a boil, cover, and braise in the oven for three to four hours.
6. The thickened cooking liquid should be served with the dish as a side dish for the geese.

Dietary Composition: Caloric Intake 260, Quantity of fat: 10g, Carbohydrate: 25g, Quantity of Fiber: 1g, Quantity of Protein: 14g

77. **Grilled Chicken with Olive Relish**

Readiness Time: 20-22 minutes Time needed to cook: 3 minutes Serve 4

Required Material:

- Chicken breast: 4
- Oil: 3/4 cup (EVO)
- Sea salt
- Freshly ground black pepper
- Capers: two tbsp
- green olives: 1 1/2 cups
- Toasted almonds, chopped: 1/4 cup
- A clove garlic, mashed together with sea salt
- Thyme: 1 1/2 tsp.
- Grated lemon zest: 2 1/2 tsp.
- Parsley: 2 tbsp.

Step-By-Step Procedure:

1. High-heat grilling is recommended.

2. Fold a sheet of plastic wrap over a single chicken breast, sprinkle with a teaspoon of olive oil, and marinate in the refrigerator for at least an hour.

3. The chicken has to be pounded with a heavy frying pan or meat mallet to an even thickness of approximately 1/2 inch.

4. Use a fresh sheet of plastic wrap and go on with with the remaining chicken.

5. Coat the chicken in approximately 2 tablespoons of extra virgin olive oil and season with sea salt and pepper; leave aside.

6. Combine the garlic, thyme, lemon zest, parsley, and extra virgin olive oil in a medium bowl and stir in the capers, olives, almonds, and the rest of the ingredients.

7. The chicken needs three minutes on each side of the grill before it can be moved to a chopping board.

8. When it has cooled, cut it into half-inch thick slices.

9. Arrange the chicken pieces and relish on four plates.

10. Dish up right away

Dietary Composition: Caloric Intake 160, Quantity of fat: 7g, Quantity of Carbohydrates: 2g, Quantity of Fiber: 0g, Quantity of Protein: 21g

78. Grilled Duck Breast with Fruit Salsa

Readiness Time: 15-17 minutes Time needed to cook: 10 minutes Quantity of Meals: 6

Required Material:

- Fruits: Plums (10), Pears (4), Nectarine (4)
- Mint leaves: 3
- A red onion
- Cracked black pepper for seasoning
- Olive oil: 1 tbsp,
- Duck breast: One and a half pounds
- Chili in powder: 1 tsp

Step-By-Step Procedure:

1. Start preheating the grill. Dice the onion, plum, peach, and nectarine into tiny cubes.

Fruit, onion, mint, and pepper are great additions.

2. In a dish, mix the oil and chili powder together.

3. Olive oil-marinated duck breast and grilled to perfection and accompanied with a dollop of salsa.

Dietary Composition: Caloric Intake 291, Quantity of fat: 11.3g, Quantity of Carbohydrates: 10.3g, Quantity of Protein: 32.6g, Quantity of Fiber: 2.2g

79. Grilled Turkey with Salsa

Readiness Time: 18-20 minutes Time needed to cook: 3 minutes Serve 6

Required Material:

- Garlic powder: half a teaspoon
- Fennel seeds: 2 teaspoons
- Paprika, sweet: 1 and a half tsp
- Dark brown sugar: two tsp
- Black pepper, freshly ground, 1 1/2 teaspoons

Salsa:

- Capers: 2 tbsp
- Cherry tomatoes: 2 scant
- Green olives: 1/4 cup
- Olive oil: One and a 1/2 tablespoons o
- Minced garlic clove: 1
- Lemon juice, freshly squeezed: 2 teaspoons
- Fresh basil leaves: 2 tbsp
- Lemon zest: 1/2 teaspoon
- Turkey breast: 6
- Red onion: one cup
- Salt of the Sea, Black Pepper

Step-By-Step Procedure:

1. In a small bowl, combine the dry spices (garlic powder, paprika, fennel seeds, brown sugar, salt, and pepper).

2. In a separate bowl, combine the capers, olives, tomatoes, onion, lemon juice, oil, lemon zest, salt, pepper.
3. To get a nice sear on both sides, grill the steak over medium heat for three minutes after dipping it in the spice rub.
4. The turkey should rest for five minutes after being removed from the grill before being served. Accompany with salsa

Dietary Composition: Caloric Intake 238, Quantity of fat: 8.4g, Quantity of Carbohydrates: 2.4g, Quantity of Protein: 33.2g

80. Quail with Plum Sauce

Readiness Time: 13-15 minutes Time needed to cook: 6 hours Quantity of Meals: 6

Required Material:

- Plums: twelve
- Quail
- Yellow onions: two
- A stalk celery
- A carrot
- olive oil: 1/4 cup + bay leaves: 2
- Dry red wine: 1 cup
- Hearty red wine brown stock: 1 quart
- Sprigs thyme, leaves only: 2
- Parsley stems: half bunch
- Kosher salt, to taste
- Fresh-cracked black pepper, to taste

Step-By-Step Procedure:

1. Peel, pit, and slice the plums; cut the quail in half; remove the breast and back bones (save the bones). The carrot should have peeled before being chopped.
2. Heat the oil in a large stockpot. Brown the quail bones in a skillet, then add the vegetables and continue cooking until the onions, carrots, and celery are transparent. It's best to add plums and wine and let the liquid shrink by half.

3. The grill is heated while stock and herbs are added and lets to boil for six hours before straining.
4. Prepare the quail by seasoning it with salt and pepper and grilling it until cooked through and golden brown.

Dietary Composition: Caloric Intake: 300, Quantity of fat: 13g, Quantity of Carbohydrates: 13g, Quantity of Protein: 30g, Quantity of Fiber: 2g

81. Roast Lemon Chicken

Readiness Time: 23-25 minutes Time needed to cook: 60-70 minutes Quantity of Meals: 4

Required Material:

- A chicken, uncut
- To taste, with salt and pepper;
- Fresh lemon juice: 2
- Extra-virgin olive oil: 2 tablespoons,
- Mustard: 1 tbsp
- Oregano: one teaspoon.

Step-By-Step Procedure:

1. Put the dish in the oven to 400 degrees.
2. You should wash the chicken and pat it dry.
3. After you've salted and peppered the interior and exterior, you may put the squeezed lemon halves inside.
4. Put chicken breasts on a rack inside a shallow baking dish. Rub the chicken all over with a mixture of lemon juice, olive oil, mint, and oregano.
5. Baste the chicken with the pan juices and flip it over halfway through the baking time (60-70 minutes).
6. Prick the meat with a fork to test doneness, or use an instant-read thermometer set to 165 degrees Fahrenheit.
7. When the chicken is done, remove it from the oven and tent it with foil. Put it in a preheated oven for ten minutes to rest.
8. Serve Hot with juices

Dietary Composition: Caloric Intake 270, Quantity of fat: 11g, Carbohydrate: 10g, Quantity of Fiber: 1g, Quantity of Protein: 31g

82. Roast Turkey

Readiness Time: 26 hours' Time needed to cook: 3 hours and 30 minutes Quantity of Meals: 10

Required Material:

- A turkey: about 12 pound (cavity and neck empty rinsed) + 3 bay leaves
- Peppercorns: 12
- Cloves garlic smashed: Three
- Sprigs fresh thyme: 6
- Thyme leaves: 1/2 teaspoon
- Fresh parsley, Moscato wine or other fortified wine: a 1-quarter cup of each
- Allspice berries: 10
- Orange juice: 1 cup
- Salt, divided: two tsp
- Oil, EVO: 1/4 mug
- Pepper: 1tsp
- Sweet paprika: half tsp
- Garlic powder, rosemary: (each) 1 tsp

Step-By-Step Procedure:

1. Put the turkey in a big enough saucepan or pail and add cold water to cover it by an inch or two. The turkey should be removed and set aside.

2. Put in the orange juice, wine, bay leaves, peppercorns, ginger, thyme, parsley, and a tsp salt.

3. Even though it takes a while, the salt in the soup will eventually dissolve if you keep stirring it. Turkey and brain should be refrigerated for a full day.

4. Put your oven up to temperature, preferably 325 degrees F. After an hour, remove the turkey from the brine and set it out at room temperature.

5. The turkey has to be washed and patted dry with paper towels. The turkey has to be roasted in a big rack.

6. Sprinkle the remaining salt, pepper, paprika, and garlic powder equally over the turkey, and then massage it all over with oil.

7. The turkey would benefit from the addition of the fresh herbs.

8. Put the turkey in the center of the oven and cook it for 3.5 hours. If the bird's skin begins to become too black, tent it with aluminum foil.

9. A meat thermometer put into the thickest part of the turkey, away from any bone, should register 180 degrees Fahrenheit.

10. Remove the turkey from the oven and tent it with foil. The recommended resting time for a cooked turkey is 45 minutes before serving.

Dietary Composition: Caloric Intake 213, Quantity of fat: 13.3g, Quantity of Carbohydrates: 0.2g, Quantity of Fiber: 0g, Quantity of Protein: 24.1g

83. Rosemary Chicken Thighs & Legs

Readiness Time: 15 minutes Time needed to cook: 1 hour Quantity of Meals: 6

Required Material:

- Chicken thighs and legs: two pounds
- Leek, prepped in the usual manner (cleaned, trimmed, halved, sliced): 1
- Garlic: a bulb of 8 cloves
- Rosemary: two tbsp

- Red potatoes that have been halved: six
- Extra-virgin olive oil: one tablespoon
- Salt: two tsp
- Pepper: three-quarters of a teaspoon
- Capers: a quarter cup

Step-By-Step Procedure:

1. Prepare a 375°F oven by turning it on. Put everything (except the capers) in a large baking dish.
2. Coat the chicken and potatoes in the marinade you just made.
3. Put the chicken on the middle rack of the oven and roast for an hour, or until an instant-read thermometer registers 180 degrees Fahrenheit.
4. Serve with a sprinkling of capers.

Dietary Composition: Caloric Intake 180, Quantity of fat: 11g, Quantity of Protein: 10g, Quantity of Carbohydrates: 0g, Quantity of Fiber: 0g

84. Slow-Cooked Duck

Readiness Time: 15 minutes Time needed to cook: 8-12 hours Quantity of Meals: 6

Required Material:

- Parsley stems: One bundle
- Bay leaves: 6
- Coarse salt: 2 tbsp
- Black pepper: one teaspoon
- Total of One bunch of thyme and sage: half of each
- Oil 1/2 mug

Step-By-Step Procedure:

1. Eliminate fat from the duck, cut the meat into serving pieces.
2. On a baking sheet, arrange the duck in a single layer. Rub the duck with the herb and spice mixture.
3. Wrap everything up with plastic. Chill in the refrigerator overnight.

4. Please wash and dry well before placing in the oven.
5. Turn the oven temperature up to 250 degrees F.
6. Oil a baking dish and set it aside. Cover and bake the duck for 8-12 hours. The duck needs to cool down for around an hour.
7. Take off the bay leaves and drain the duck well to separate the oil.
8. Place the duck on a pan under the broiler and cook until browned. Now serve.

Dietary Composition: Caloric Intake 558, Quantity of fat: 34g, Quantity of Carbohydrates: 0g, Quantity of Protein: 58g

85. Slow Cooker Rosemary Chicken

Readiness Time: 15 minutes Time needed to cook: 7-hours Quantity of Meals: 8

Required Material:

- A single tiny onion
- Smashed garlic cloves: four
- Green or yellow peppers: one
- Rosemary: 2 tsp
- Pork sausages: 2
- Dried oregano: a half teaspoon
- Coarsely powdered pepper: 1/4 teaspoon
- Dry vermouth: 1/4 cup
- Chicken breast: 8
- Corn starch: 1 1/2 tbsp
- Cold water: 2 teaspoons

Step-By-Step Procedure:

1. In a slow cooker, combine the onions, garlic, pepper, rosemary, and oregano.
2. Take the sausages out of their casings and break them into the dish.
3. Pepper the chicken and put it flat in a layer over the sauce.
4. Cook with vermouth for 7 hours on low heat.

5. Get out a deep tray and set the chicken in it.
6. To thicken the liquid in the slow cooker, mix the cornstarch with the water in a small dish.
7. Increase the temperature and cover. Ten minutes of marinating is recommended.

Dietary Composition: Caloric Intake 278, Quantity of fat: 10g, Carbohydrate: 8g, Quantity of Fiber: 1g, Quantity of Protein: 33g

86. Spicy Turkey Breast with Fruit Chutney

Readiness Time: 20 minutes Time needed to cook: 1 hour and 10 minutes Quantity of Meals: 6

Required Material:

- Cloves garlic: 2
- Jalapeno peppers: two
- Olive oil: one tbsp worth
- Flour of any kind: 2 tsp
- Black pepper, to taste, freshly cracked
- Spray for the oven
- Turkey breast: 1 1/2 pounds
- A Lemon
- Shallot 1
- Pears: 2 sliced
- Honey: one tablespoon's worth

Step-By-Step Procedure:

1. Get the oven ready at 350 degrees.
2. Remove the seeds and stems from the peppers, then chop them. You can make a delicious sauce by blending garlic, olive oil, and chili peppers. It's best to mix the flour with the ground black pepper.
3. Spray a cooling rack with cooking spray. Put the turkey on a rack after dredging it in flour, then dipping it in pepper.
4. Bake for an hour with the foil lightly covering the dish. For the last 10 minutes of cooking, discard the foil.

5. The shallots for the chutney should be diced very finely. Lemon juice has a tangy and pleasant flavor.
6. Mix the sliced pears with the lemon juice, zest, honey, and zested shallots.
7. Serve the turkey with thin slices and chutney.

Dietary Composition: Caloric Intake 290, Quantity of fat: 4.5g, Quantity of Carbohydrates: 24g, Quantity of Fiber: 2g, Quantity of Protein: 34g

87. Turkey Breast Piccata

Readiness Time: 22 minutes Time needed to cook: 8-10 minutes Quantity of Meals: 6

Required Material:

- Turkey breast: One and a half pounds
- All-purpose flour: one-fourth cup
- EVO oil: one-fourth cup
- Lemon juice, fresh: (3 tbsp)
- Dry white wine: A quarter mug
- Turkey or chicken stock: Half a cup
- Parsley: 1/4 cups
- Capers: 1/2 tbsp

Step-By-Step Procedure:

1. Make scallion-sized slices of turkey breast and dredge them in flour. In a large skillet, heat the oil for 30 seconds over medium heat.
2. The turkey should broil for two minutes after being sliced.
3. Reduce the wine by half, then stir in the lemon juice. After adding the stock, continue cooking for another 5-6 minutes, or until the sauce thickens.
4. Before serving, sprinkle the capers and parsley over the turkey slices and then top with the sauce.

Dietary Composition: Caloric Intake 170, Quantity of fat: 5g, Quantity of Carbohydrates: 8g, Quantity of Protein: 24g, Quantity of Fiber: 0g

88. Turkey Burgers

Readiness Time: 17 minutes Time needed to cook: 15-20 minutes Serve 4

Required Material:

- Egg, only white: 1
- Red onion: one cup
- Mint: ¾ cup
- Dried bread crumbs: half cup
- Dill: 1 tsp.
- Feta cheese: 3/4 cup
- Turkey, ground: Three-quarter kg
- Cooking spray
- Hamburger buns: four
- A red bell pepper, roasted and cut in strips
- Lime juice: 2 tbsp.

Step-By-Step Procedure:

1. After mixing the egg white, onion, mint, dill, cheese, turkey, and lime juice together, the turkey mixture should be split into four equal burger patties.
2. Heat the cooking spray in a large nonstick skillet over medium heat.
3. Cook the patties for 8 minutes each side, or until they reach the desired doneness, taking care not to break them apart. When the sausages are done, pile them over the bread halves and top with pepper slices. Serve

Dietary Composition: Caloric Intake 585, Quantity of fat: 33.6g, Quantity of Carbohydrates: 24.7g, Quantity of Protein: 47.2g, Quantity of Fiber: 9.1g

89. Warm Chicken Avocado Salad

Readiness Time: 21 minutes Time needed to cook: 8-10 minutes Serve 4

Required Material:

- EVO oil: 2 tbsp.
- Fillets of Chicken breast: 500 g.
- A medium-sized avocado, chopped after peeling
- Minced garlic cloves: two
- Turmeric in powder: 1 tsp
- Cumin Powder: Three Tablespoons
- One head broccoli
- Diced Carrots: 1 Large
- Currants: 1/3 mug
- Chicken stock: about 1 1/2 cups
- Sea salt, to taste,
- Couscous: one and a half cup

Step-By-Step Procedure:

1. Chicken: In a large skillet, heat 1 tablespoon of extra-virgin olive oil over medium heat.
2. Cover and allow stand for 5 minutes or until all of the liquid has been absorbed after stirring boiling stock into the currants and couscous.
3. You may separate the grains using a fork.
4. Cook the carrots in the remaining oil for approximately a minute, stirring often.
5. After 1 minute, add the garlic, turmeric, and cumin and stir to combine.
6. After another minute, take the pan from the stove.
7. In a large bowl, mix the broccoli and chicken; toss to incorporate; season with salt; and finish with a dollop of avocado.

Dietary Composition: Caloric Intake 200, Quantity of fat: 10g, Quantity of Protein: 24g, Quantity of Carbohydrates: 1g.

SEAFOOD

90. Baccalà

Readiness Time: 24 hours' Time needed to cook: 10 minutes Quantity of Meals: 6

Required Material:

- Baccalà (salted cod): Half a pound
- A couple of plum tomatoes
- Garlic: 3
- A celery stalks
- Parsley: 1/2 bunch
- Oil of olive: one Tbsp
- White wine: 1/4 cup
- Fish stock 1/2 mug
- Freshly black pepper

Step-By-Step Procedure:

1. Put the baccalá in water for a day.
2. Put down the garlic! Cube the tomatoes and celery to about the same size.
3. Prepare a big sauté pan with oil and heat it over medium heat.
4. Sauté the bacon for approximately a minute on each side before adding the garlic, tomatoes, and celery.

5. After adding the wine, the volume is reduced by about half.
6. Stir in the stock and seasonings; cook on low for 10 minutes, covered, and serve with the cooking liquid and some parsley.

Dietary Composition: Caloric Intake 571, Quantity of fat: 29g, Quantity of Carbohydrates: 19g, Quantity of Protein: 50g, Quantity of Fiber: 1g

91. Cioppino

Readiness Time: 25 minutes Time needed to cook: 1-hour Quantity of Meals: 6

Required Material:

- Clams
- Mussels: 1 pound (scrubbed, debearded)
- Cod fillet: 1 ½ pounds
- A shallot
- Yellow onion: one
- Garlic, celery salks, carrots: Two pieces of each
- Plum tomatoes: 3
- Wine, white: 1 mug
- Fish Stock: 3 mugs
- Saffron threads: 1 tsp
- Dried red pepper flakes: 1/4 teaspoon
- Oil: 1/2 teaspoon
- Capers: 1/4 teaspoon

Step-By-Step Procedure:

1. Use extremely cold water to clean the clams.
2. Thoroughly scrub the mussels. Break the cod into manageable chunks. Cut the celery, onion, shallot, and garlic into small

cubes. Cut the carrots and tomatoes into tiny cubes after peeling them.

3. Simmer the fish, vegetables, wine, stock, saffron, and pepper flakes for an hour in a large saucepan.
4. Put the mussels in the pot and boil them until they open.
5. Season the cioppino with garlic powder and drizzle with olive oil. Serve.

Dietary Composition: Caloric Intake 250, Quantity of fat: 0g, Quantity of Carbohydrates: 12g, Quantity of Protein: 25g, Quantity of Fiber: 1g

92. Cod with Raisins

Readiness Time: 24 hours' Time needed to cook: 1-hour Quantity of Meals: 4

Required Material:

- Salted cod: 1 1/2 pounds
- extra-virgin olive oil: 3 or 4 tablespoons
- Cooking onions: two
- Tomato paste: 1 tablespoon diluted in 3/4 cup water
- Black raisins: 3/4 cup
- Water: 1 cup

Step-By-Step Procedure:

1. Throughout at least 24 hours, with frequent water changes, soak salted fish in the water to eliminate salt. In a saucepan, warm the olive oil over medium heat.
2. Add onions for flavor and a quick sauté. Don't stop stirring until the onion is the perfect blend of soft.
3. Simmer the onions in the tomato paste for 10 minutes after bringing to a boil.
4. After adding the water, continue cooking for a further three minutes.
5. Put in some water, bring to a boil, and then let it simmer for half an hour, or until the droplets have grown.
6. Simmer the fish in the sauce for 15 minutes after reducing the sauce by half. Drizzle with sauce and serve.

Dietary Composition: Caloric Intake 140, Quantity of fat: 1.5g, Quantity of Carbohydrates: 8g, Quantity of Protein: 25g, Quantity of Fiber: 0.5g

93. Grilled Calamari

Readiness Time: 15 minutes Time needed to cook: 2-3 minutes Quantity of Meals: 4

Required Material:

- Squid, cleaned:4 (5-inch-long)
- Extra-virgin olive oil: 1/4 cup
- A clove garlic minced
- Salt: one tsp
- Pepper: 1/2 teaspoon
- Vegetable oil: 3 tablespoons
- Fresh lemon: two tbsp only juice
- Dried oregano: 1/2 tsp

Step-By-Step Procedure:

1. Prepare a grill with medium heat, whether using gas or charcoal. Put oil, garlic, salt, and pepper into a medium bowl and stir until combined.
2. To oil the grill, just wipe it down with a clean tea towel that has been soaked in vegetable oil. Squid needs around three minutes on the grill each side.
3. The all is best served hot with a drizzle of lemon juice and a sprinkling of chopped fresh oregano.

Dietary Composition: Caloric Intake 97, Quantity of Protein: 16.2 g, Quantity of fat: 1.2g, Carbs: 5.9g, Quantity of Fiber: 0.3g

94. Grilled Grouper Steaks

Readiness Time: 1 hour and 24 minutes Time needed to cook: 5-6 minutes Quantity of Meals: 4

Required Material:

- Oil type extra-virgin: one quarter cup
- Grated lemon zest: One tBsp

- White wine: half mug
- Rosemary: half tsp
- Grouper steaks: four
- Vegetable oil: 3 tablespoons
- Salt: 1 1/2 teaspoons

Step-By-Step Procedure:

1. In a medium baking dish, combine the oil, zest, wine, and rosemary. Fish should both be included.
2. After plastic wrapping, refrigerate for an hour. Before being grilled, fish should sit out at room temperature for 30 minutes.
3. Grill using medium heat, either gas or charcoal.
4. To oil the grill, just wipe it down with a clean tea towel that has been soaked in vegetable oil.
5. Apply salt to both sides of the fish.
6. Cook the fish on a hot grill for about 5-6 minutes each side.
7. Serve.

Dietary Composition: Caloric Intake 218, Quantity of fat: 6g, Quantity of Carbohydrates: 0g, Quantity of Protein: 38g, Quantity of Fiber: 1g

95. Grilled Jumbo Shrimps

Readiness Time: 25 minutes Time needed to cook: 2-3 minutes Quantity of Meals: 4

Required Material:

- Virgin olive oil: 1/4 cup
- Salt: 3/4 teaspoon
- Pepper: One-quarter teaspoon
- A pinch of paprika, sweet
- Shrimp: 12
- Butter: Half a cup
- Fresh lemon juice: two Tbsp
- A minced and peeled garlic clove
- Flake red pepper: about 1/8 teaspoon
- Ginger: one tsp
- Chives and parsley: a tbsp of each
- Oil type vegetable: 3 tbsp

Step-By-Step Procedure:

1. Prepare a gas or charcoal fire by heating it to medium-high and then brushing it down well.
2. Whisk together the olive oil, salt, pepper, and paprika in a medium bowl. Add the shrimp and marinate for 10 minutes.
3. Combine the butter, lemon juice, garlic, red pepper flakes, and ginger in a small saucepan and let it melt over low heat. Place some chives and parsley in the dish. The sauce should be kept at a warm temperature.
4. When the grill is ready, wipe it down with a clean tea towel that has been dipped in vegetable oil.
5. Grill the shrimp for two minutes on each side, or until an instant-read thermometer registers 145 degrees Fahrenheit.
6. Butter sauce should be used sparingly on the shrimp.
7. Served on the side.

Dietary Composition: Caloric Intake 140, Quantity of fat: 1g, Quantity of Protein: 23g, Quantity of Carbohydrates: 1g, Quantity of Fiber: 1g

96. Grilled Lobster

Readiness Time: 20 minutes Time needed to cook: 4-6 minutes Quantity of Meals: 4

Required Material:

- Live lobsters, split lengthwise: 4
- EVO Oil: 2/3 cup + 1quarter cup
- Salt: 1 1/2 teaspoons
- Pepper: 1/2 teaspoon
- Sweet paprika: 3 quarter tsp
- A clove garlic
- Lemon juice: 2 Tbsp
- Dijon mustard: 1 1/2 tablespoons
- A scallion
- Parsley + oregano: a total of two tbsp
- Vegetable oil: 3 tablespoons

Step-By-Step Procedure:

1. By using gas or charcoal, heat the grill to medium. Clean the grill grates thoroughly with a brush.
2. Sprinkle a teaspoon each of salt, pepper, and paprika over the flesh side of the lobster and rub with a quarter cup of olive oil. You may retain half the rules for yourself if you cut them in half.
3. To make the dressing, in a medium bowl, mix the remaining oil with vinegar, lemon juice, mustard, scallions, parsley, oregano, and salt. Prepare the sauce separately. When the grill is ready, rub the surface with vegetable oil using a clean tea towel.
4. The grilling time for lobster claws is longer, so start with them. Minutes later, with the meat side down, set the lobster bodies on the grill.
5. Turn the bodies and claws after three or four minutes on the grill. Continue grilling for another 2–3 minutes, or until the shells become red and the meat is no longer pink in the middle.
6. The sauce should be drizzled over the lobsters, and any leftovers should be served on the side.

Dietary Composition: Caloric Intake: 200, Quantity of fat: 4g, Quantity of Carbohydrates: 0g, Quantity of Protein: 36g, Quantity of Fiber: 0g

97. Grilled Octopus

Readiness Time: 20 minutes Time needed to cook: 1-hour Quantity of Meals: 4

Required Material:

- Octopus, already cleaned: Three pounds
- Bay leaves: 3
- red wine: 1/4 mug
- Balsamic vinegar, divided: 3 Tbsp
- oil type extra-virgin olive: 2/3 cup
- Pepper, Oregano and salt: you need 1 tsp of each
- A large lemon, cut into wedges.

Step-By-Step Procedure:

1. Put the octopus and bay leaves in a large saucepan and cook over medium heat. Cover and simmer the octopus for around 5 to 8 minutes.
2. Take off the cap and measure how much liquid (in cups) the octopus has released.
3. Cook for a further 5 minutes with the lid on, or until the octopus has released its liquid. Cook the octopus over medium-low heat for 45 minutes, or until soft.
4. Add the 2 tablespoons of vinegar to the wine. Turn off the heat and allow the octopus cool in the liquid until it reaches room temperature.
5. Grill using medium heat, either gas or charcoal. Take the octopus out of the liquid and chop it apart, being careful to separate the tentacles.
6. Combine the octopus, oil, oregano, and remaining wine in a large bowl. Season to taste with salt and pepper.
7. The octopus should be grilled for two to three minutes each side.
8. Garnish the grilled octopus with the remaining olive oil and serve with lemon wedges.

Dietary Composition: Caloric Intake 121, Quantity of Protein: 26g, Quantity of fat: 1.6g, Carbs: 4g, Quantity of Fiber: 1g

98. Grilled Salmon with Lemon and Lime

Readiness Time: 15-17 minutes Time needed to cook: 7-10 minutes Quantity of Meals: 4

Required Material:

- Fillet of salmon: 4 (6-ounce)
- Oil of olive (EVO): 1/4 cup
- Grated lemon zest: one Tbsp
- Grated lime zest:1 1/2 teaspoons
- Pepper: 1/2 teaspoon
- Vegetable oil: 3 tablespoons
- Salt: 1 1/2 teaspoons
- A large lemon, cut into wedges

Step-By-Step Procedure:

1. Prepare on a gas or charcoal grill set to medium heat.
2. Use a brush with firm bristles to scrub the grill surface clean.
3. You need to clean the fillets by rinsing them and drying them with a paper towel.
4. Season the fillets with salt and pepper and sprinkle with lemon and lime zest after applying olive oil to both sides.
5. Vegetable oil on a clean tea towel may be used to wipe down the grill before you start cooking.
6. For around seven minutes, salmon are best-grilled skin-side down. Don't mess with the fillets while they're grilling. After two or three minutes, flip and return to the grill.
7. Serve the salmon with slices of lemon.

Dietary Composition: Caloric Intake 203, Quantity of fat: 8.8g, Quantity of Carbohydrates: 0.7 g, Quantity of Protein: 29.2 g, Quantity of Fiber: 0 g

99. Grilled Sardines with Wilted Arugula

Readiness Time: 15-17 minutes Time needed to cook: 3-6 minutes Quantity of Meals: 4

Required Material:

- Sardines: sixteen (fresh)
- Baby arugula: two huge bunches
- Pepper, sea salt, and lemon wedges
- Oil EVO: 2 tsp

Step-By-Step Procedure:

1. The outside grill or griddle has to be fired up. Rinse the arugula under cold running water, shake off any excess water, and arrange the leaves in a single layer on a serving dish.
2. To remove the scales, simply wash the sardines in running water, rub them together, and then pat them dry before adding them to a large bowl of extra virgin olive oil.
3. Cook the sardines on a hot grill for three minutes each side, or until they are crisp and golden.
4. Season with salt and pepper and move to an arugula-lined dish right away. Garnish with lemon slices and serve right away.

Dietary Composition: Caloric Intake 300, Quantity of fat: 20g, Quantity of Protein: 20g, Quantity of Carbohydrates: 10g, Quantity of Fiber: 3g

100. Grilled Sea Bass

Readiness Time: 10-13 minutes Time needed to cook: 15 minutes Quantity of Meals: 4

Required Material:

- Whole sea bass: 4
- Salt & pepper
- Pure olive oil: One-quarter cup
- Oregano, dry: one teaspoon
- Parsley: 1 cup

Step-By-Step Procedure:

1. Completely gut and rinse the fish. Make a lot of diagonal incisions on both sides of each fish using a sharp knife.
2. Season with salt and pepper on the inside and exterior, then leave aside while you prepare the rest of the ingredients.
3. Thinly slice the remaining two lemons and arrange a few slices and some chopped parsley on top of each plate.
4. After 10 minutes, brush the fish with olive oil and sprinkle it with the lemon mixture. Oil the grill and heat it to medium. Position fish fillets on the grill rack and cover to cook.
5. Cook in oil until salmon flakes, about 15 minutes.
6. Make a paste with the remaining olive oil and lemon juice and serve it hot...

Dietary Composition: Caloric Intake 230, Quantity of fat: 6g, Quantity of Carbohydrates: 0g, Quantity of Protein: 40g, Quantity of Fiber: 1g

101. Grilled Tuna

Readiness Time: 15-17 minutes Time needed to cook: 6 minutes Quantity of Meals: 4

Required Material:

- Tuna steaks: 4 pieces
- Hickory wood chips: a 1/2 cup
- Black pepper
- Sea salt
- A lime juices
- Extra virgin olive oil: three Tbsp

Step-By-Step Procedure:

1. Seal the plastic bag with the tuna and olive oil and place it in the refrigerator for at least an hour.
2. Prepare the grill, whether using charcoal or gas.
3. Hickory wood chips added to hot coals on a charcoal barbecue enhance the meat's taste. Lightly grease the grill racks.
4. Grill the tuna for 6 minutes total, flipping once, and seasoning with salt and pepper.
5. Immediately after cooking, serve the fish with a squeeze of lime.

Dietary Composition: Caloric Intake: 110, Quantity of Protein: 25g, Quantity of fat: 2g,

Quantity of Carbohydrates: 0g, Quantity of Fiber: 0g

102. Halibut Roulade

Readiness Time: 2 hours Time needed to cook: 4-5 minutes Quantity of Meals: 6

Required Material:

- Fillet of halibut: One-pound
- Shrimp: 1/2 pound; Limes: 3
- Cilantro: A quarter bunch
- Garlic: 3
- Leek: 1/2, Olive oil: 1 Tbsp
- Seafood. reduction demi-glaze sauce: just 1 mug

Step-By-Step Procedure:

1. It's recommended to soak 12 wooden skewers in water for at least two hours before using them. The grill should be heated up beforehand.
2. Get the fish clean and put it in the fridge. Shrimp shells and tails should be removed (but saved for potential later use). The shrimp should be deveined and halved lengthwise. Take two limes, remove their zest, and juice them. To garnish, cut the remaining lime into six wedges and lay aside six full cilantro leaves. Thinly slice the leek and chop the garlic.
3. To achieve a fillet thickness of between 1/2 and 3/4 inches, cut butterfly the halibut fillet along its length. The fillet should be laid out and the shrimp, half the lime zest, half the cilantro, the garlic, and the leeks should be added.
4. Roll the packed fillet into a log and carefully cut it into six equal pinwheels. Each pinwheel should have an X-shaped pair of skewers inserted into it to prevent it from breaking. Oil the grill grates and cook the fish for 4 minutes on each side.
5. Pepper and any residual citrus zest and cilantro may be sprinkled on top. Use the remaining oil and the reducing sauce to drizzle over the top...

Dietary Composition: Caloric Intake 383, Quantity of fat: 17g, Quantity of Carbohydrates: 6g, Quantity of Fiber: 0g, Quantity of Protein: 50g

103.   Mediterranean Cod

Readiness Time: 20-23 minutes Time needed to cook: 35 minutes Quantity of Meals: 4

Required Material:

- A single table scoop of pure olive oil
- Frozen Onion, 100g
- Garlic, minced: one tablespoon
- Tomatoes from Italy: 230g can
- Tomato purée: 1 tbsp.
- Cod fillets 400g
- Frozen mixed peppers: 200g.
- Frozen parsley: one TBSP
- black olives: 50 g
- Cooked white rice: Eight hundred g

Step-By-Step Procedure:

1. The onion should be sautéed in a skillet with extra virgin olive oil over medium heat for about three minutes.
2. Two minutes after the scent has developed, add the garlic. Bring the water, tomato puree, and chopped tomatoes to a low boil and stir.
3. To thicken, reduce heat and simmer, uncovered, for 20 minutes.
4. Place the fish in the sauce and gently prod it with a spoon. The sauce should be brought back to a boil, then simmered for 8 minutes at low heat. Add the parsley and olives and cook for a further two minutes.
5. While waiting, prepare some rice according to the package's instructions. Accompany fish with hot rice.

Dietary Composition: Caloric Intake: 96, Quantity of Carbohydrates: 0g, Quantity of fat: 2g, Quantity of Protein: 20g, Quantity of Fiber: 0g

104.   Octopus in Wine

Readiness Time: 15-17 minutes Time needed to cook: 30-35 minutes Quantity of Meals: 4

Required Material:

- A big octopus
- White vinegar: One Tbsp
- Oil: 1/2 cup
- Onions: Three
- Tomatoes: 4
- White wine: 1 cup
- Bay leaves: 2
- Peppercorns, whole: one teaspoon
- To season with salt and pepper
- Capers: 1/2 cups, drained
- Water: a quarter mug

Step-By-Step Procedure:

1. For fifteen until twenty minutes, or until tender, cook the octopus in a covered pot over low heat. Remove and finely dice them.
2. Before adding the tomatoes, wine, bay leaves, peppercorns, salt, and pepper to the onions that have been sautéed in olive oil until tender, boil the mixture for 15 minutes.
3. Add the octopus and capsicum and cook until the sauce has thickened.
4. Remove the bay leaves and serve immediately.

Dietary Composition: 142, Quantity of fat: 4.3g, Quantity of Carbohydrates: 5.1g, Quantity of Fiber: 0.2g, Quantity of Protein: 20.2g

105.   Oysters on the Half Shell

Readiness Time: 20-23 minutes Time needed to cook: 0 minutes Quantity of Meals: 4

Required Material:

- Fresh Oysters: Sixteen
- Crushed Ice: 4 Cups

- A Big Lemon

Step-By-Step Procedure:

1. Lay one oyster on a flat surface, hinge side up, then prop it up with a tea towel using one hand. With your other hand, carefully put a knife or oyster shucker into the hinge. The shell may be opened by placing the knife into the hinge and wiggling it inside.
2. Slide the knife over the top of the shell to cut through it and reach the muscle below.
3. The ability to shuck an oyster is essential. A card should be placed on top. To remove an oyster from its shell, just slide the knife under it. Remove the debris and shards of shell.
4. Inhale the oyster's scent; it should take you back to the ocean. So be it if it doesn't work. The remaining fish should go through the same steps.
5. Place them on a bed of crushed ice and garnish with lemon slices to serve.

Dietary Composition: Caloric Intake: 69, Quantity of Carbohydrates: 2.5g, Quantity of fat: 1.3g, Quantity of Protein: 9g, Quantity of Fiber: 0g

106. Pistachio-Crusted Halibut

Readiness Time: 15-18 minutes Time needed to cook: 25 minutes Quantity of Meals: 4

Required Material:

- Pistachios: 1/2 cups, shelled and unsalted, finely chopped
- Zest of lemons: 2 Tsp
- Lime, grated: a single tsp
- Orange zest: 2 tsp
- Fresh parsley, chopped: (about 4 tablespoons' worth)
- Halibut fillets: 4 (about six ounces total)
- Bread Crumbs: One Cup
- Virgin olive oil: a quarter of a cup
- Season with Salt: 1 1/2 teaspoon
- Pepper: half Tsp

- Dijon mustard: 4 tsp

Step-By-Step Procedure:

1. The ideal oven temperature is 400 degrees Fahrenheit. Pistachios, zest, parsley, and bread crumbs may be mixed together in a food processor by using the "pulse" option. It's best to add the oil and thoroughly blend it in while the processor is running.
2. Cleaning fish entails rinsing it and patting it dry with paper towels.
3. Season the fish with salt and pepper just before serving. Run the blade of the sword along the fish's fins.
4. Sprinkle the pesto mixture liberally over the fish. Pressing down on the mixture improves crust adherence.
5. Place the coated fish in a single layer on a baking sheet lined with parchment paper. Put it on the center rack in the oven and bake it for 20 minutes, or until the crust is golden.
6. Give the fish 5 minutes to chill off before serving.

Dietary Composition: Caloric Intake 387, Quantity of fat: 15g, Quantity of Carbohydrates: 31g, Quantity of Protein: 28g, Quantity of Fiber: 4g

107. Roasted Sea Bass Potatoes and Fennel

Readiness Time: 18-20 minutes Time needed to cook: 50 minutes Quantity of Meals: 2

Required Material:

- Medium potatoes: four
- A small onion
- Parsley: 2 tablespoons
- A cup thinly sliced fennel
- lemon zest, grated: 1 1/2 teaspoons
- Lemon juice: 1 tablespoon + 1/3 mug
- oil, divided: Two tbsp
- Salt: Two tsp
- Pepper: 1 teaspoon

- Basic vegetable stock: half cup
- Tomatoes, sliced: two
  Whole European sea bass: 1/2-pound
- Fennel fronds: 6 TBSP
- Scallions: 4 (softened in boiling water for 10 seconds)
- Kalamata olives: eight
- Caper berries, rinsed: four
- Wine: 1-quarter cup
- One lemon

Step-By-Step Procedure:

1. Turn the oven temperature up to 450 degrees F. In a medium baking dish, combine the potatoes, onions, parsley, fennel, lemon zest, and lemon juice. Combine a third of a cup of oil. One teaspoon of salt and half a teaspoon of pepper should be stirred into the stock to season it.
2. Place the tomatoes over the fennel and potatoes. Put the rack in the middle of the oven and bake for 25 minutes.
3. While waiting, clean the fish by rinsing it and drying it with a paper towel. Season both sides and the inside of the fish's cavity with salt and pepper, then rub the remaining oil all over the fish. Sprinkle two onions around each fish and stuff two teaspoons of fennel fronds into each cavity.
4. Once the veggies are done, take them out of the oven and place the salmon on top. It's a good idea to sprinkle olives and caper berries on top. Fill the fish and veggies to the brim with wine. Bake in the middle of the oven for 20–25 minutes, or until the fish is cooked through and the potatoes are soft.
5. Place the fish on top of the cooked veggies, and use the leftover fennel fronds and lemon wedges for decoration.

Dietary Composition: Caloric Intake 450, Quantity of fat: 20g, Quantity of Carbohydrates: 50g, Quantity of Protein: 30g, Quantity of Fiber: 5g

108. Salmon and Haddock Terrine

Readiness Time: 20 minutes Time needed to cook: 1-hour Quantity of Meals: 6

Required Material:

1. Olive oil: A single tablespoon
2. Salmon fillet and haddock fillet: 3/4 pound of each
3. Garlic: three
4. A medium eggplant
5. Fresh-cracked black pepper, to taste
6. Kosher salt, to taste
7. A head arugula
8. Roasted Red Peppers: 2

Step-By-Step Procedure:

1. Prepare an oven temperature of 375 degrees F. Grease a loaf pan with olive oil.
2. Use cold water to clean the fish, then pat it dry.
3. Make paper-thin slices of garlic. After being half lengthwise, eggplant has to be roasted for 20 minutes.
4. Put some salt and pepper on the fish. Salted eggplant, arugula, haddock, cooled red peppers, garlic, should be layered on a preheated pan.
5. Take 20 minutes to bake after being securely wrapped in foil.
6. Press down on the stacked contents after removing the wrapper, then rewrap firmly and bake for another 10-20 minutes.
7. Take it out of the oven and let it cool in the fridge overnight.
8. Take off the mold from the loaf pan just before serving.

Dietary Composition: Caloric Intake 340, Quantity of fat: 21g, Quantity of Carbohydrates: 4g, Quantity of Protein: 34g, Quantity of Fiber: 0g

109. Sautéed Red Snapper

Readiness Time: 20 minutes Time needed to cook: 4-5 minutes Quantity of Meals: 6

Required Material:

- Red snapper, fresh: 1 1/2 pounds
- Turmeric: 1/4 teaspoon
- Curry powder: A single teaspoon
- Garam masala: a quarter tsp
- Oil: two tbsp
- Fresh-cracked black pepper, to taste
- Unbleached flour, for all use: one mug
- Buttermilk and nonfat yogurt: (each) a quarter cup

Step-By-Step Procedure:

1. The fish must be washed in cold water and patted dry. Make six separate fish entrées. Sift together the flour, turmeric, curry powder, garam masala, black pepper, and salt. In another container, mix the buttermilk and yogurt together.
2. Fish should be dusted in the flour mixture, dipped in the yogurt mixture, and then returned to the flour mixture.
3. To prepare the fish, heat the oil in a large sauté pan over medium heat. Once hot, add the fish and cook until golden brown and flaky on both sides.

Dietary Composition: Caloric Intake 124, Quantity of fat: 2g, Quantity of Carbohydrates: 0g, Quantity of Protein: 25g, Quantity of Fiber: 0g

110. Sea Bass Baked with Coarse Sea Salt

Readiness Time: 18-20 minutes Time needed to cook: 30 minutes Quantity of Meals: 2

Required Material:

- Whole sea bass: one-pound
- Some fresh thyme: maybe three to four sprigs
- Parsley, fresh: half a cup
- Egg whites: 3 (beaten)
- Lemon: 1 + zest grated 1 tbsp
- Cold water: a half-cup
- Ladolemono: 1/2 mug
- Coarse sea salt: 2 teaspoons;
- Flour for all use: 1/3 cup

Step-By-Step Procedure:

1. Reduce the heat to 450 degrees F. in the oven. Please wash and dry thoroughly using a paper towel.
2. Stuff the fish with some thyme, parsley, and lemon slices.
3. Combine the salt, flour, eggs, and zest in a medium bowl and stir to combine. Adding water gradually while stirring will create a paste. There's a chance you won't need all that water; the paste shouldn't flow too freely.
4. On a baking sheet large enough to hold the entire fish, spread a layer of the salt mixture (approximately a third of the total). Place the fish on top of the salt, head first, and cover it with the remaining salt mixture, being careful to leave the tail and fins visible. To ensure the salt stays down, pack it down. Bake in the middle of the oven for 30 minutes. Wait 10 minutes before serving the fish.
5. The fish may be revealed by gently cracking the salt crust with a hammer or the flat side of a meat tenderizer. After scraping off the salty skin with the back of a knife, carefully invert the fish onto a serving dish. Take off the opposite side's skin. Dollop some of the lemon sauce on top of the fish and serve the remainder on the side.

Dietary Composition: Caloric Intake 200, Quantity of fat: 5g, Quantity of Carbohydrates: 0g, Quantity of Protein: 33g

111. Steamed Snow Crab Legs

Readiness Time: 20-23 minutes Time needed to cook: 40-45 minutes Quantity of Meals: 6

Required Material:

- Snow crab claw clusters: six
- Parsnips: 2 pounds
- Celery stalks: 6
- A yellow onion
- Parsley: half bunch
- White wine (Pinot Grigio or Sauvignon Blanc): 1/2 mug
- Juice of lemon: one
- Fish Stock: 1 cup
- Bay leaves fresh: 3 - cracked black pepper

Step-By-Step Procedure:

1. The crab legs need to be washed in very cold water. Parsnips should have their rinds removed and be chopped coarsely. Roughly chop the celery and onion. Prepare the kale by chopping it.
2. Bring everything except the snow crab to a boil in a medium-sized saucepot, then decrease heat to a simmer, covering the pot and cooking for another 20-30 minutes.
3. Crab legs may be cooked for as little as 10 minutes or as long as 15 minutes. Remove the bay leaves and serve.

Dietary Composition: Caloric Intake 70, Quantity of fat: 1g, Quantity of Carbohydrates: 0g, Quantity of Protein: 15g, Quantity of Fiber: 0g

112. Tilapia with Smoked Gouda

Readiness Time: 21 minutes Time needed to cook: 40-45 minutes Quantity of Meals: 6

Required Material:

- Fresh Tilapia fillets: 1 1/4 ounces
- Plum tomatoes, fresh: 6
- Garlic: 3
- A leek - turnips
- Shallot: 1
- Gouda, Smoked: 3 ounces
- Sprigs of parsley: 1-quarter
- Olive oil: one tbsp's worth
- Fish stock: a single mug
- Wine type red: a quarter cup
- Cracked black pepper for seasoning

Step-By-Step Procedure:

1. Preheat the oven to 375 degrees F.
2. Use cold water to clean the fish, then pat it dry. Cube the tomatoes into bite-sized pieces. You should thinly slice peeled turnips. Cut the leek into extremely thin slices. Prepare the shallots and garlic by chopping them. Prepare the kale by chopping it. The cheese is appreciated.
3. In an olive oil-coated baking dish, arrange the fish fillets, leeks, potatoes, shallots, and garlic. After adding the stock and wine, cook covered for 30 to 40 minutes.
4. Locate and top with sliced tomatoes and grated cheese. To ensure the cheese melts fully, re-ignite the oven. Serve immediately when hot, topped with parsley and pepper. Select a dry wine with enough character to compete with the smoked cheese. Red wines that are easy to drink and not too heavy are a great match with fish.

Dietary Composition: Caloric Intake 200, Quantity of fat: 8g, Quantity of Carbohydrates: 3g, Quantity of Protein: 25g, Quantity of Fiber: 0g

MEAT, BEEF & PORK

113. Braciola

Search for steaks that are rough ⅛" thick, 8"– 10" long, and 5" wide to make this Italian dish.

Readiness Time: 20 minutes Time needed to cook: 1-2 hours Quantity of Meals: 8

Required Material:

- Oil: ½ tsp
- Onion: ½ cup
- Garlic, minced: two
- Tomatoes: 1 (32-ounce) can
- Stalks rapini: eight
- Exceptionally flimsy cut round steaks: 8 (about 1¼ pounds complete)
- Bread scraps and Parmesan cheese: Four Tsp of each

Step-By-Step Procedure:

1. Oil should be heated in a big, nonstick frying pan over medium heat.
2. For approximately 5 minutes, or until the onions are tender, sauté the onions and garlic in the olive oil. Put in a large oval slow cooker (about 6 quarts in size).
3. Tomatoes will stay together better if you blend them well. Steaks should be placed on a flat serving platter next to trimmed rapini.

4. Sprinkle each steak with a quarter of a teaspoon of bread crumbs and a quarter of a teaspoon of Parmesan.
5. Each steak should have a generous amount of rapini leaves placed on one side. Each steak has to be wrapped lengthwise so that the rapini filling may fit snuggly within. A spiral form is required.
6. Place in a big skillet fold side down.
7. Put in a pan and cook for 1 second over medium heat. Flip the steaks carefully and allow them complete cooking for a further minute on the other side.
8. Toss the tomato puree into a slow cooker and arrange the rolls on top in a single layer. After 1 to 2 hours in a low oven, steaks should be done cooking.

Dietary Composition: Caloric Intake: 500, Quantity of fat: 20g, Quantity of Carbohydrates: 18g, Quantity of Protein: 32g, Quantity of Fiber: 1g

114. Cheddar Stuffed Bifteki

Readiness Time: 4 hours' Time needed to cook: 10 minutes Serve 8

Required Material:

- Hamburger of beef: Two pounds
- Onions: 2
- Bread (Crushed by hand after being soaked in water): 3 slices
- Minced Garlic One TBsp
- Oregano: one teaspoon
- New parsley: one teaspoon
- Allspices: A Half-Teaspoon
- Pepper: about a tsp
- Graviera cheddar: Eight (1-ounce) blocks

Step-By-Step Procedure:

1. Throw the meat, onions, bread, garlic, rosemary plant parsley, allspice, salt, and

pepper into a big bowl and mix everything together.

2. Form the ground beef into 16 patties, each measuring 4 by 1.5 inches. The patties should be chilled for at least 4 hours and up to overnight after being placed on a dish and covered securely with plastic wrap.
3. Burger patties should be brought to room temperature before being grilled.
4. Insert a piece of cheddar cheese into the center of a burger.
5. Just stack another patty on top and squeeze it together to make a burger.
6. Seal the burger by squeezing it tightly between your fingers.
7. Light a gas or charcoal grill to medium-high heat.
8. The secret to excellent barbecue is a good brushing.
9. When the grill is hot, wipe it down with a clean tea towel soaked in vegetable oil, add the burgers, and cook for 5 minutes each side.

Dietary Composition: Caloric Intake 400, Quantity of fat: 30g, Quantity of Carbohydrates: 5g, Quantity of Protein: 25g, Quantity of Fiber: 1g

115. **Fasolakia with Veal**

Readiness Time: 20 minutes Time needed to cook: 1 hour and 5 minutes Quantity of Meals: 4

Required Material:

- Oil: 1/3 mug
- onions, peeled and sliced: three
- garlic: 5, peeled and sliced
- parsley: half mug
- mint: 1/4 cup
- dill: 1/2 cup
- Fasolakia: (runner beans: 2 pounds
- Tomatoes: 3 skinned and grated
- Salt
- Veal or beef, already cooked: 2 pounds
- A pinch pepper
- Large potatoes: 2

- Hot veal broth: about 3 cups

Step-By-Step Procedure:

1. Put the oil in a big pan and heat it for 30 seconds over medium heat.
2. It should take around 5 minutes of cooking time for the onions to get tender.
3. Add the tomatoes, beans, garlic, parsley, mint, dill, and a pinch of salt.
4. Over high heat, bring the ingredients to a boil; then, decrease the heat to medium and cook for 30 minutes.
5. Season to taste with salt and pepper.
6. The dish needs veal, potatoes, and enough liquid to cover everything.
7. If you want soft potatoes and a little thicker sauce, simmer for another 30 minutes.
8. Season to taste with salt and pepper immediately. Do not wait to serve.

Dietary Composition: Caloric Intake 400, Quantity of fat: 15g, Quantity of Carbohydrates: 20g, Quantity of Protein: 20g

116. **Green Curry Beef**

Readiness Time: 34-40 minutes Time needed to cook: 40 minutes Serve 3

Required Material:

- EVO oil: just a tbsp.
- Parsley: ½ cup
- Cilantro: 1 cup
- White onion: one
- A fresh Thai green chili, chopped
- Garlic, thinly sliced: 2 cloves
- Turmeric: Half tsp (divided)
- Lime juice: 2 tbsp.
- Salt of sea¼ tsp.
- Black pepper
- Beef top round: 16 oz.
- A can light coconut milk
- A quarter tsp turmeric
- Cumin: A single tsp (divided)

Step-By-Step Procedure:

1. *The first step is to prepare the curry sauce:* you will have to mix together oil, parsley, cilantro, onion, chili pepper, garlic, half the turmeric and the cumin, lime juice, a pinch sea salt, and pepper
2. *Now prepare Meat:* Toss the meat and green curry paste together in a bowl.
3. Put in the fridge and chill for at least half an hour.
4. When you're ready, put the beef and green curry sauce in a big pan and cook it over medium heat.
5. Ten minutes of browning the meat's outside at a low temperature with occasional stirring should enough.
6. Add the coco milk. To thicken the sauce, let it simmer for approximately 30 minutes while stirring periodically.
7. Promptly serve

Dietary Composition: Caloric Intake 350, Quantity of fat: 20g, Quantity of Carbohydrates: 15g, Quantity of Protein: 30g, Quantity of Fiber: 3g

117. Healthy Lamb Burgers

Readiness Time: 16 minutes Time needed to cook: 10 minutes Serve 4

Required Material:

- A single tablespoon of pure olive oil
- Yogurt cheese fat-free: 2 tbsp
- Cured lamb meat, ground: 1 pound
- Ground allspice: ⅛ tsp.
- Cilantro leaves,: half cup
- A small egg, only white
- Cloves garlic: two
- Ginger, minced and fresh: 2 tsp.
- A red chili pepper
- Cumin: ⅛ tsp. (ground)
- Cardamom seeds: 4
- A shallot, finely chopped
- Black pepper: 1/8 teaspoon
- Salt of sea: a quarter

- Spray olive oil
- Whole-wheat hamburger buns: four

Step-By-Step Procedure:

1. Put everything in the fridge for at least 20 minutes to let the flavors meld, except the spray olive oil and the buns.
2. Raise the temperature to 400 degrees Fahrenheit on your oven's thermostat.
3. Extra virgin olive oil should be warmed over medium heat in a large, nonstick pan. Meanwhile, make four burgers out of the lamb mixture.
4. Burgers should be seared for twenty seconds on each side in a hot pan before being transferred to an oven that has already been prepared.
5. Flip the burgers after five minutes and cook for another three.

Dietary Composition: Caloric Intake 535, Quantity of fat: 22g, Quantity of Carbohydrates: 35g, Quantity of Protein: 44g, Quantity of Fiber: 5g

118. Herb-Maple Crusted Steak

Readiness Time: 14 minutes Time needed to cook: 10 minutes Serve 4

Required Material:

- For each aromatic herb (rosemary, fresh tarragon, oregano, chives): use 3 tbsp.
- Parsley: 4 tbsp.
- Maple syrup: three Tbsp
- Ribeye steaks, trimmed: 4 (4 ounce)
- Sea salt: ½ tsp.
- Pepper: ¼ tsp.
- spray olive oil

Step-By-Step Procedure:

1. Start by preheating the oven to 450 degrees Fahrenheit.
2. Heat an oven-safe, nonstick pan. While you wait, mix the chopped herbs on a dish. Separate a basin for the maple syrup.

3. Prepare the steak by seasoning it with sea salt and pepper, then dipping it in maple syrup before cooking it.
4. Coat the steak well by dipping each side of it into the herb mixture.
5. Apply the same method to the remaining steak. Spray some extra virgin olive oil onto the hot pan as soon as you remove it from the oven.
6. To ensure uniform browning, add the steaks and turn them over once.
7. Four minutes each side in a hot oven, then six minutes overall

Dietary Composition: Caloric Intake 250, Quantity of fat: 25g, Quantity of Carbohydrates: 10g, Quantity of Protein: 25g, Quantity of Fiber: 2g

119. Lemon Verbena Rack of Lamb

Readiness Time: 21 minutes Time needed to cook: 35 minutes Quantity of Meals: 4

Required Material:

- Lamb racks, with the silver skin removed and tied: weighing a total of 2 pounds
- Smashed cloves of garlic: 2
- Olive oil: a quarter cup
- Mustard: 1 tablespoon
- Sweet paprika: one teaspoon
- Honey: a single TBsp.
- Parsley: Two tablespoons
- Lemon, only zest: Two teaspoons
- Lemon verbena leaves: 2 tablespoons
- Fresh thyme: 2 tablespoons
- Salt: 3 Teaspoons
- Pepper: just one tsp

Step-By-Step Procedure:

1. Place the lamb in an oven-safe dish of about the same size.
2. Fill a food processor with the olive oil, garlic, mustard, paprika, honey, lemon zest, parsley, lemon verbena, and thyme. Keep going until everything is evenly combined.

3. The lamb has to marinate, so pour the marinade over it and massage it all over. Lamb has to be marinated for an hour at room temperature in a covered dish. Salt and pepper the meat and set it aside.
4. Get the broiler going. Arrange the lamb in a single layer on a baking sheet covered with parchment paper, and broil for 5 minutes. Roast the meat for 25 minutes at 450 degrees Fahrenheit.
5. Lamb should be cooked to an internal temperature of 135 degrees Fahrenheit.
6. If you want your lamb well done, roast it for a few more minutes.
7. Let the lamb rest for five minutes in foil before serving.
8. The rack of lamb will need to be trimmed and the silver skin removed by the butcher. Then, he'll quickly prepare the lamb by tying it into a crown rack.

Dietary Composition: Caloric Intake 610, Quantity of fat: 36g, Quantity of Carbohydrates: 3g, Quantity of Protein: 62g, Quantity of Fiber: 0g

120. Lemony Pork With Lentils

Readiness Time: 8 hours' Time needed to cook: 30 minutes Serve 4

Required Material:

- Pork chops, four (4 oz.)
- Extra-virgin olive oil: 2 teaspoons
- Squeezed lemon juice, fresh: 2 tbsp. + Zest: a single tsp
- A clove of garlic
- Fresh sprigs of rosemary, minced: Two TBSP
- Parsley and Pure maple syrup: (each) 1 tbsp
- Green lentils: about 1/2 cup
- Water: about 6 mugs.
- A celery rib and 1 shallot
- Sherry, dry: 1/2 cup
- Red pepper flakes: a quarter tsp
- Salt, Table: a single tsp
- Butter, without salt: 1 Teaspoon

Step-By-Step Procedure:

1. Marinate the pork chops in a resealable plastic bag for at least eight hours in a mixture of extra virgin olive oil, and syrup.
2. Green lentils need 20 minutes of cooking time in a pot with 3 cups of water over medium heat.
3. Turn on the oven to its highest setting, which is 3500 F. Sear the pork for two minutes on each side in a hot, nonstick pan over medium heat, then finish it off in the oven.
4. Cook the shallot, red pepper flakes, and celery in 1 tablespoon of extra-virgin olive oil in a separate nonstick skillet over medium heat.
5. Toss in the lentils, and toss until warm. Two minutes into cooking time, stir in a pinch of sea salt and a quarter cup of sherry.
6. During that period, the volume of the liquid should decrease by half. Melt the butter by stirring it in.
7. On each of four dishes, top the lentil mixture with a pork chop from the first pan. Take the first fillet out of the marinade, toss the garlic, and add a quarter cup of sherry to the pan to deglaze it.
8. Raise the temperature and mix in a pinch of salt. Reduce the liquid by half while cooking.
9. Serve by evenly distributing the sauce over the food.

Dietary Composition: Caloric Intake 600, Quantity of fat: 20g, Quantity of Carbohydrates: 50g, Quantity of Protein: 30g, Quantity of Fiber: 15g

121. Liver with Apple and Onion

Readiness Time. 14 minutes Time needed to cook: 20 minutes Serve 2

Required Material:

- Extra virgin olive oil spray
- Onion: ½ lb.
- Granny Smith apples: two
- Water: A single cup
- Juice of fresh lemon: A TBSP
- White wine Vinegar: a single tbsp.
- brown sugar: one tsp.
- Rosemary: 1 tbsp + sprigs for garnish
- Currants: 2 tbsp.
- Butter, without salt: 2 tsp.
- Calves' liver: 8oz
- White wine: a quarter mug
- Sea salt: a pinch
- Olive oil spray

Step-By-Step Procedure:

1. Turn up the oven's heat to a scorching 200 degrees Fahrenheit in advance.
2. Steak is sprayed with olive oil spray and cooked over medium heat for 4 minutes while onions are sautéed till transparent.
3. Apples need around 5 minutes in the oven to start browning.
4. Cook the apples in water, vinegar, sugar, and lemon juice until the apples are fork-tender.
5. After two minutes, mix in the butter until it foams, then pour half onto each of two dishes and keep warm in the oven.
6. Toss in the chopped liver and cook for 10 minutes, or until it has a browned exterior.
7. Spread the apple-onion mixture on two plates, then divide the liver between them.
8. Deglaze the skillet by adding white wine and letting it simmer down until it's reduced by half.
9. Then spoon the sauce over the individual portions. Serve with a sprig of fresh rosemary.

Dietary Composition: Caloric Intake 134, Quantity of fat: 5.2g, Quantity of Carbohydrates: 7.2g, Quantity of Protein: 16.2g, Quantity of Fiber: 1.7g

122. Meatballs with Mushrooms

Readiness Time: 26 minutes Time needed to cook: 3-4 hours Quantity of Meals: 6

Required Material:

- Patties of lean beef: One-pound
- A minced clove of garlic
- Celery: 1/4 cup
- Uncooked rice: 1/2 cup
- Bread scraps: One-half cup
- Sage: 1/2 teaspoon
- A pinch of salt and white pepper: a total a tsp
- Mushrooms: 1/2 pound
- vegetable oil: 3 tablespoons
- A large onion, peeled and chopped
- Universally Flour: 1 Tablespoon
- Tomato paste: A cup
- Water: One mug

Step-By-Step Procedure:

1. To prevent food from sticking to the bottom of the pot, spray the interior with nonstick cooking splash.
2. Roll mixtures of ground beef, garlic, celery, rice, bread crumbs, savvy, salt, and pepper into balls about 4 inches in diameter.
3. Two tablespoons of oil should be heated over medium heat in a big skillet. Brown the meatballs for about a minute on each side, using a dish lined with paper towels. Careful preparation in advance is required to make meatballs in a slow cooker.

4. The last tablespoon of oil may be heated in a large pan over medium heat. Mushrooms and onions take around 5 minutes total to cook in a sauté pan. Add flour to the mushroom mixture and whisk to thicken. Blend the tomato puree and water until there are no chunks left.
5. Simmer the meatballs in the tomato-mushroom sauce for three to four hours on low heat, covered.

Dietary Composition: Caloric Intake 250, Quantity of fat: 20g, Quantity of Carbohydrates: 15g, Quantity of Protein: 20g, Quantity of Fiber: 3g

123. Mediterranean Beef Pitas

Readiness Time: 15 minutes Time needed to cook: 2-3 minutes Serve 4

Required Material:

- Ground beef: One pound
- Black pepper & sea salt
- Oregano: 1 ½ tsp.
- Oil (EVO): 2 Tbsp
- A small red onion: used just 1/4
- Hummus: 3/4 cup
- Pitas:4
- Lemon: 4 slices
- One bunch of flat-leaf parsley: about Two Tbsp

Step-By-Step Procedure:

1. Season 1/4 teaspoon of ground peppercorns 1/2 teaspoon of sea salt, and 1/8 teaspoon of oregano into the meat, then form into 16 patties.
2. Cook the beef patties in a pan with 1 tablespoon of extra-virgin olive oil over medium heat for approximately 2 minutes each side, or until browned.
3. Beef patties, hummus, parsley, and onion should be placed on pitas, and then the pitas should be drizzled with the remaining extra virgin olive oil and garnished with lemon wedges.

Dietary Composition: Caloric Intake 350, Quantity of fat: 8g, Quantity of Carbohydrates: 45g, Quantity of Protein: 14g, Quantity of Fiber: 5g

124.   Moussaka

Readiness Time: 25 minutes Time needed to cook: 1 hour Quantity of Meals: 10

Required Material:

- Salt: 2 tbsp.
- Eggplants: three big
- Oil olive: Two tablespoons of high-quality
- Breadcrumbs: 1 cup
- Greek meat marinade: six mugs
- Romano cheese: One and a half cups
- Béchamel sauce: Four cups

Step-By-Step Procedure:

1. Eggplant slices benefit from being marinated in salt for 30 minutes before being cooked. To dry the egg plants, use a paper towel. Turn on the oven and set the temperature to 400 F.
2. Brush the eggplants with oil and spread them out on an oiled baking sheet. The eggplants just need 6 minutes in the oven to soften. (The eggplant works well on the grill, too.) Before letting the eggplants cool, put them to a tray lined with paper towels to absorb any remaining oil. Reduce the temperature in the oven to 375 degrees F.
3. Spread some of the eggplant slices out in the bottom of a large casserole. Wrap the eggplant in half a cup of breadcrumbs. Spread half of the Greek Meat Sauce over the bread crumbs. Then, add half a cup of grated cheese. Spread another layer of eggplant, half a cup of cheese, the remaining breadcrumbs, and Greek meat sauce.
4. Béchamel sauce should be used to cover the moussaka. The last 30–40 minutes of baking time should be spent melting and browning the remaining cheese.

5. Wait 45 minutes to slice and serve the moussaka.

Dietary Composition: Caloric Intake: 350, Quantity of fat: 30g, Quantity of Carbohydrates: 20g, Quantity of Protein: 20g, Quantity of Fiber: 5g

125.   Osso Buco

Readiness Time: 26 minutes Time needed to cook: 2-3 hours Quantity of Meals: 10

Required Material:

- Veal Shanks: 5 pounds
- Salt: two tsp
- Pepper, ground: 1 teaspoon (split)
- Virgin olive oil: a tbsp
- A leek (with ends removed, washed, trimmed, cut in half lengthwise, and sliced),
- Big tomatoes: Three
- Onions and garlic: (each) four
- Basil: 3 cups
- Red wine: A cup
- Beef or veal stock: three cups
- Bay leaves: Two
- Parsley: three tablespoons
- Fresh thyme and fresh rosemary: each measuring to a tbsp.

Step-By-Step Procedure:

1. Get the oven going at 325 degrees Fahrenheit and on. Use 1 teaspoon of salt and 1/2 teaspoon of pepper to season the shanks.
2. Oil should be warmed for 30 seconds in a covered Dutch oven set over medium heat. It's time to throw in some shanks and do a quick roast for three or four minutes on each side.
3. Vegetables such as leeks, tomatoes, onions, garlic, celery, and carrots should be added. Do a quick roast on the veggies. Toss in the wine and reduce it by half over a two- to three-minute simmer.

4. Mix in some stock, fresh herbs (such as parsley, thyme, and rosemary), and bay leaves. The veal should be brought to a boil, then covered and cooked in the oven. After two to three hours in the braising liquid, the meat should be soft enough to break away from the bone. Take down the bay leaves.
5. You may eat it hot, or you can let it cool, store it in the fridge, and reheat it the following day.

Dietary Composition: Caloric Intake 590, Quantity of fat: 24.5g, Quantity of Carbohydrates: 8.3g, Quantity of Protein: 63.5g, Quantity of Fiber: 2.3g

126.   Parmesan Meat Loaf

Readiness Time: 17 minutes Time needed to cook: 50 minutes Serve 4

Required Material:

- Diced flat-leaf parsley: 1/2 cup
- Beef, ground: 1 1/2 pounds
- A big egg
- Bread crumbs: half cup
- Minced onion: one
- Grated Parmesan: half cup
- Tomato paste: about 1/4 cup
- Cracked black pepper

Step-By-Step Procedure:

1. Turn the oven up to 4000F. In a large bowl, mix together all the components.
2. Put the meat mixture into a loaf pan lined with foil (the pan should be 8 inches in diameter).
3. Pre-heat oven to 350 degrees and bake for 50 minutes, stirring occasionally.

Dietary Composition: Caloric Intake 250, Quantity of fat: 15g, Quantity of Carbohydrates: 10g, Quantity of Protein: 25g, Quantity of Fiber: 2g

127.   Pork Souvlaki

Readiness Time: 5 hours; Time needed to cook: 3-4 minutes Quantity of Meals: 8

Required Material:

- Peel and grate one big onion.
- Garlic cloves: Three
- Salt: 2 tsp.
- Boneless pork butt: Two pounds
- Lemons: two
- Pepper: 3-quarter teaspoon
- Oil type vegetable: 1-quarter cup plus three tablespoons
- Oregano: four teaspoons
- Salt: two tsp

Step-By-Step Procedure:

1. In a large bowl, combine the onion, garlic, salt, pepper, 1/4 cup oil, and oregano with a whisk. The goal is to create a perfect marinade by combining all of the ingredients. Coat the meat with the pork and potatoes. At a minimum, pork has to be chilled for 5 hours, and ideally, overnight. The pork has to be at room temperature before being grilled.
2. Put the meat on skewers made of wood or metal. Put four pork cubes on each skewer.
3. Prepare a grill medium fire using gas or charcoal. Brush the grill surface well to remove any residue and provide a clean cooking surface.
4. As soon as the grill is done, use a clean tea towel dipped in the leftover oil to wipe out the surface. Cook the pork for three to four minutes on each side, or until it reaches an internal temperature of 165 degrees Fahrenheit.
5. Serve the pork with the remaining oregano and lemon wedges.

Dietary Composition: Caloric Intake: 300, Quantity of fat: 12g, Quantity of Carbohydrates: 24g, Quantity of Protein: 24g, Quantity of Fiber: 2g

128. Roast Pork Belly and Potatoes

Readiness Time: 21 minutes Time needed to cook: 50 minutes Quantity of Meals: 12

Required Material:

- Potatoes Yukon Gold: about 10
- EVO oil, stock (hot chicken, turkey or basic vegetable): each 1/2 cup
- Dijon mustard: 2 tablespoons
- A tablespoon lemon juice
- Sprigs fresh thyme plus: ten
- Thyme leaves: 2 teaspoons
- 2 or 3 sprigs fresh rosemary
- Salt: 3 teaspoons (divided)
- Pepper, divided: 1 1/2 teaspoons
- Pork belly: 1 (31/2-pound
- Sweet paprika: 2 teaspoons
- Oregano: 1 teaspoon
- Bacon: 1/4 cup
- A head garlic

Step-By-Step Procedure:

1. Put the dish in the oven and preheat it to 400 degrees F.
2. In a roasting pan, combine the potatoes with the olive oil, stock, mustard, lemon juice, thyme, and rosemary. to coat potatoes in the mixture, combine the ingredients.
3. Toss in a teaspoon of salt and a half a teaspoon of pepper. Reserve.
4. In a large bowl, combine the pork belly with the rest of the salt, the rest of the pepper, the paprika, the oregano, and the thyme leaves. Combine all of the ingredients and toss in the pork.
5. The belly pork should be placed above the spuds. Scatter the smoked pork over the potatoes and belly.
6. Make room in the middle of the skillet for the garlic.
7. After 30 minutes of baking on the middle rack, the pork should be uniformly browned.

8. After 20 minutes, or when the meat is browned and the potatoes are soft, turn the pork over and return it to the oven. Dish up right away.

Dietary Composition: Caloric Intake: 700, Quantity of fat: 50g, Quantity of Carbohydrates: 30g, Quantity of Protein: 50g, Quantity of Fiber: 3g

129. Sausage Patties

Readiness Time: 15 minutes Time needed to cook: 2-3 minutes Quantity of Meals: 6

Required Material:

- Pancetta and pork fat: 4 ounces (each 2 oz)
- Pork, already ground: 1/2 pound
- Veal: 1/2 pound ground
- A egg
- Black pepper: a tbsp
- Sage: 1 tablespoon
- Red pepper flakes: 1/4 tsp
- A tsp ground cumin
- Kosher salt, to taste
- Olive oil: one

Step-By-Step Procedure:

1. Pancetta and pork fat need to be coarsely chopped. Mix all the ingredients together (except the oil) until uniform, then form into patties.
2. A pan with oil in it should be heated over medium heat.
3. Brown the patties on all sides and keep them covered to ensure they cook through.
4. Serve after draining on a paper towel-lined rack.

Dietary Composition: Caloric Intake: 189, Quantity of fat: 11.7g, Quantity of Carbohydrates: 0g, Quantity of Protein: 16.9g, Quantity of Fiber: 1g

130. Short Ribs with Red Wine

Readiness Time: 22 minutes Time needed to cook: 6-8 hours Quantity of Meals: 6

Required Material:

- Short ribs of hamburger: 1½ pounds
- A tablespoon cumin
- Thyme: 1 teaspoon
- Foe each (garlic in powder, salt, onion in powder): Half teaspoon
- Dark pepper: just a tsp
- olive oil: One tablespoon
- Enormous red onions: two
- Huge plum tomatoes, hacked: twelve
- red wine: a single cup
- Vegetable Broth: 4 Cups

Step-By-Step Procedure:

1. Season the ribs with a variety of herbs and spices, including salt, pepper, onion particles, garlic powder, thyme, cumin, and others.
2. After browning the ribs for approximately 5 minutes on each side in a Dutch oven over medium heat, transfer the browned ribs to a slow cooker.
3. Add the onions to the Dutch broiler after 2 minutes and continue cooking until they are transparent. Use wine as a deglazing agent, then reduce the heat to low and wait until the liquid has evaporated, about 10 minutes.
4. Cook until the liquid reaches a simmer. Simmer the ribs in the wine sauce for 6 to 8 hours, covered. To thicken the sauce, take the cover off the slow cooker and cook it on high for 15 minutes.

Dietary Composition: Caloric Intake: 600, Quantity of fat: 40g, Quantity of Carbohydrates: 15g, Quantity of Protein: 50g, Quantity of Fiber: 2g

131. Special Veal and Mushrooms

Readiness Time: 16 minutes Time needed to cook: 10-12 minutes Quantity of Meals: 6

Required Material:

- Olive oil: 2 tablespoons
- Veal cutlets: 1½ pounds
- Salt: ½ teaspoon
- Separated, dark pepper: 1½ teaspoons
- Mushrooms, cut: 1-pound
- Garlic: 6
- Arugula: 4 mugs
- Wine (red) and Stock for hamburger: each Half cup
- Olives: a quarter mug

Step-By-Step Procedure:

1. Put 1 tablespoon of oil into a large pan and heat it over medium heat. The cutlets just require a minute in the pan after being seasoned on both sides with salt and half a teaspoon of pepper. Remove the veal from the heat, but maintain it at a warm temperature.
2. Add the remaining oil and reduce the heat to medium. The mushrooms, garlic, and arugula should be cooked in a flash for 2 minutes. Before adding the stock, let the wine simmer for a minute. Keep simmering for another ten minutes.
3. Lay mushrooms to a serving platter. Veal cutlets on the mushrooms. When ready to serve, top with olives and a dash of pepper.

Dietary Composition: Caloric Intake: 200, Quantity of fat: 7g, Quantity of Carbohydrates: 1g, Quantity of Protein: 31g

132. Slow-Roasted Leg of Lamb

Readiness Time: 26 minutes Time needed to cook: 2 hours and 50 minutes Quantity of Meals: 10

Required Material:

- Lam leg: about 6-8 ounces with bone in
- A head garlic, bulbs peeled and cut thin
- Extra-virgin olive oil: three Tbsp
- Salt: 5 Tsp + Pepper: Two Tsp
- Garlic powder: 2 tsp
- Oranges, medium: you need Two
- Sweet paprika: two tsp
- Rosemary, fresh sprigs: Two or three
- Sprigs thyme: ten
- White wine and hot water: a total of 1 cup
- Oregano: 2 tsp
- Bay leaves: 3
- Squeezed lemon juice: 1/3 mug

Step-By-Step Procedure:

1. Using a paring knife, make a small hole in the lamb and insert a garlic clove. To get as many garlic slices into the leg as possible, repeat the technique as many as required.
2. Turn the oven temperature up to 550 degrees Fahrenheit. After massaging the lamb with the 3 tablespoons of oil, place it in a roasting pan that is just big enough to accommodate it. Mix together salt, pepper, garlic powder, and paprika, then rub all over the meat.
3. Lamb needs to roast for around 10–15 minutes uncovered. Ten to fifteen minutes more, or until browned, if roasting the lamb on the opposite side. Reduce the heat to 350 degrees F. in the oven.
4. The onions, rosemary, thyme, oregano, and any remaining bay leaves should be thrown into the roasting pan. To the lamb, you should add some lemon juice, wine,

and boiling water until it is covered by about a third. Cover and roast the lamb for two hours, basting once an hour.

5. Roast the lamb for another hour after turning it over. If extra boiling water is needed, keep cooking the lamb until it is thoroughly browned, the bone is exposed, and the flesh is starting to separate from the bone.
6. Put away the bay leaves, please. Basting and letting lamb lie for 15–20 minutes brings forth its greatest flavor.

Dietary Composition: Caloric Intake: 221, Quantity of fat: 17g, Quantity of Carbohydrates: 0g, Quantity of Protein: 22g, Quantity of Fiber: 0g

133. Steak Sandwiches Mushrooms, Cheddar

Readiness Time: 13 minutes Time needed to cook: 15 minutes Serve 4

Required Material:

- Superior Quality Olive Oil: Two Tbsp
- A clove of garlic, minced
- Cremini mushrooms, sliced: one cup
- Salt: 1/4 teaspoons
- Thyme: Half a teaspoon
- Rosemary: A half teaspoon
- Melitzano Salad: Half a Cup
- Sandwiches: four buns
- Pepper dark: 1/8 tsp
- Grilled flank steak, thinly cut: 1-pound
- Powdered Provolone cheese: equaling 1/2 cup

Step-By-Step Procedure:

1. Raise the temperature to 450 degrees F.
2. Sauté the garlic, mushrooms, salt, and pepper in the oil for 30 seconds in a medium saucepan.
3. After 8-10 minutes in the oven, mushrooms will soften. Turn off the heat and toss in some thyme and rosemary. Wait.

4. The bottom bread of each sandwich will be covered with Melitzano Salata, and the flank steak will go on top. Steak tastes great topped with cheese and a mushroom combination.
5. The sandwiches may be heated in the microwave for 5 minutes, without the top bun, or until the cheese has melted.
6. Served hot, each sandwich is wrapped in foil.

Dietary Composition: Caloric Intake 575, Quantity of fat: 28g, Quantity of Carbohydrates: 39g, Quantity of Protein: 34g, Quantity of Fiber: 4g

134. Stifado (Braised Beef with Onions)

Readiness Time: 15 minutes Time needed to cook: 1 hour Quantity of Meals: 4

Required Material:

- Stewing meat, cut into cubes: 2 Pounds
- Tomato paste: equivalent to 2 tbsps diluted in 2 cups water.
- Wine vinegar (or a sweet dessert wine like Madeira): two tablespoons
- Peeled pearl onions: Sixteen
- Peeled garlic cloves: 6
- Spice cloves: four
- A cinnamon stick
- Oregano, dried: one tablespoon
- Pepper and salt, ground to order

Step-By-Step Procedure:

1. In a large skillet over medium heat, brown the meat on both sides by adding the olive oil and flipping it often to avoid sticking.
2. Over high heat, mix together the tomatoes paste, wine vinegar, onions, garlic, cloves, cinnamon, oregano, salt, and pepper.
3. Reduce the temperature to medium and keep for about an hour.
4. Quick service is required with the fresh bread and sauce.

Dietary Composition: Caloric Intake: 450, Quantity of fat: 25g, Quantity of Carbohydrates: 25g, Quantity of Protein: 30g, Quantity of Fiber: 3g

VEGETARIAN AND LEGUMES

135.   Baked Gigantes Beans

Readiness Time: 20-23 minutes Time needed to cook: 1 hour and 40 minutes Quantity of Meals: 8

Required Material:

- Great northern beans: 16 oz
- A big carrot + one long stalk of celery
- Bay leaves: 3
- Peeled and crushed garlic cloves: 4
- EVO oil: 1/2 cup
- Onions: two
- tomato sauce: 1/2 cup + Tomato paste (1.5 tablespoons);
- Smoked paprika :(1 teaspoon)
- A pinch of salt, a dash of pepper
- Dill: a quarter cup
- A cup parsley

Step-By-Step Procedure:

1. Set oven to 350 degrees. The beans should be cooked in a large pot. Put in enough water to completely submerge the beans in the pot.
2. After the water has come to a boil, turn the heat down to medium and let it simmer for two minutes.
3. Put the beans back into the emptied can. We recommend adding garlic, bay leaves, carrots, and celery.
4. Water should cover the contents by about an inch in the saucepan. The beans should be cooked for around 45 minutes at a boil, then reduced heat to medium.
5. Remove the saucepan from the heat and set it aside.
6. Oil should be heated for 30 seconds in a big skillet over medium heat. After approximately 5 minutes, add the onions and boil them down until they are tender but not browned.
7. Mix in the tomato sauce, paste, seasonings, and herbs. Position the panful forward.
8. Put the bean and vegetable mixture into a large casserole dish using a slotted spoon. The onion mixture should be lay into the beans very gently.
9. Pour enough of the saved liquid into the casserole dish to cover the contents.
10. Add more salt and pepper to taste if required. For 30–35 minutes at 350 degrees, cook.
11. After removing the casserole from the oven, add the dil and mix well.
12. For a further 10 to 15 minutes, or until the liquid has evaporated and the top is a deep golden brown, return the dish to the oven.
13. Serve!

Dietary Composition: Caloric Intake 240, Quantity of fat: 2g, Quantity of Carbohydrates: 40g, Quantity of Protein: 12g, Quantity of Fiber: 15g

136. Barbecued Fennel

Readiness Time: 15-17 minutes Time needed to cook: 10 minutes Quantity of Meals: 4

Required Material:

- Fennels: Two
- Olive oil: the total amount is 1 tablespoon.
- Red pepper & salt: each 1/8 teaspoon
- An Orange
- Almonds, uncooked: one-fourth cup

Step-By-Step Procedure:

1. Initiate a grill over moderate heat.
2. Grill the fennel bulbs for 4 to 6 minutes each side after cutting them in half lengthwise, brushing them with olive oil, seasoning them with salt and red pepper flakes, then grilling them.
3. Use a sharp knife to remove the orange's peel and the white pith within. Separate the orange halves by cutting it in half lengthwise.
4. Toast the almonds in a skillet over medium heat for three to four minutes, turning or moving them often to avoid scorching. The orange segments need to be garnished with ground almonds.
5. Combine the fennel, orange segments, and almonds that have been coarsely chopped. You may drizzle with the olive oil on top. Serve.

Dietary Composition: Caloric Intake 155, Quantity of fat: 6g, Quantity of Carbohydrates: 17g, Quantity of Protein: 4g, Quantity of Fiber: 5g

137. Braised Okra with Tomato

Readiness Time: 15 minutes Time needed to cook: 15-20 minutes Quantity of Meals: 6

Required Material:

- Okra: around 1.5 pounds
- Tomatoes: 8 plum
- Shallots: two
- Feta cheese: four ounces
- Oregano: four sprigs
- Olive oil: one Tbsp
- Wine: one-fourth cup (dry red)
- Basic vegetable stock: half a cup
- Cracked black pepper for seasoning.

Step-By-Step Procedure:

1. The oven has to be preheated to 375 degrees F.
2. Remove the tops off the okra. Cut the tomatoes into wedges. Shallots and garlic should be minced or chopped very finely.
3. Over medium heat, warm the oil in a Dutch oven (or other heavy-bottomed pans with a cover). For two minutes, sauté the onion, garlic, and ginger.
4. The recipe should be halved after the wine is added.
5. Throw in some oregano and chicken stock, bring to a boil, cover, and bake for 15 to 20 minutes.
6. Take it out of the oven, sprinkle some feta cheese on top, and season it with pepper.
7. Serve.

Dietary Composition: Caloric Intake 119, Quantity of fat: 3.6g, Quantity of Carbohydrates: 20.3g, Quantity of Protein: 3.2g, Quantity of Fiber: 4.1g

138. Broiled Broccoli and Tomatoes

Readiness Time: 15-17 minutes Time needed to cook: 15 minutes Quantity of Meals: 4

Required Material:

- Broccoli: A pound
- Roma or cherry tomatoes: 2 cups
- Oil: 4 tsp
- Balsamic vinegar: 2 tablespoons' worth.
- Sugar or honey: no more than a quarter teaspoon
- Oregano: one teaspoon dry
- A clove of garlic, minced
- A pinch of salt

Step-By-Step Procedure:

1. Raise the oven's temperature to 450 degrees Fahrenheit to get ready for the broiler.
2. Each broccoli crown should have its florets removed, leaving a 1-inch stem. Remove the additional tail with a vegetable peeler and cut it into pieces approximately an inch long.
3. To soften broccoli in the microwave, combine it with a quarter cup of water in a microwave-safe dish and heat on high for three minutes.
4. Broccoli should be mixed with quartered tomatoes. Prepare a baking dish for the veggies and sprinkle with olive oil.
5. Broil the broccoli for 12-15 minutes, or until a light brown color develops on the stalks.
6. Add sugar, oregano, garlic, and balsamic vinegar to a bowl and stir to combine. Remove the vegetables from the broiler and immediately mix them with the balsamic dressing on a serving dish.
7. Dish out and eat.

Dietary Composition: Caloric Intake 178, Quantity of fat: 7g, Carbs: 13g, Quantity of Protein: 9g, Quantity of Fiber: 4g

139. Curry-Cooked Cauliflower

Readiness Time: 16 minutes Time needed to cook: 35 minutes Quantity of Meals: 6

Required Material:

- One-headed carrot
- Olive oil: a quarter mug
- Vinegar, preferably red: half mug
- Powdered coriander: 1 teaspoon
- Powdered cumin seeds: one teaspoon
- Curry Powder: 1 TBSP
- Paprika: One Tablespoon
- Salt: 1 teaspoon

Step-By-Step Procedure:

1. Make sure your oven's broiler is preheated to 425 degrees.
2. Cauliflower (with leaves and stems) should be chopped and placed in a medium basin. The remaining ingredients may be combined in a small bowl with a whisk. Spread the sauce over the cauliflower and mix it.
3. Combine the cabbage and sauce and bake for 35 minutes. Serve

Dietary Composition: Caloric Intake 55, Quantity of fat: 2g, Quantity of Carbohydrates: 8g, Quantity of Protein: 3g, Quantity of Fiber: 3g

140. Eggplant Parmesan

Readiness Time: 21 minutes Time needed to cook: 30-40 minutes Quantity of Meals: 10

Required Material:

- Extra-virgin olive oil: 1/2 cup with more for frying
- Medium onions: two
- Minced, peeled cloves of garlic: 6-8
- Pepper & salt: a tsp + 2 tsp
- Tomato paste: Two 28-ounce cans
- Standard Flour: One Cup
- Eggs: Four
- Big eggplants: 2
- Bread crumbs: 3 cups
- Parmesan: 1/2 cup
- Fresh basil leaves: 1 1/4 cups
- Cheese: mozzarella slices: 16

Step-By-Step Procedure:

1. After heating the oil for 30 seconds over medium heat, add the onions, garlic, 1 teaspoon of salt, and 1/2 teaspoon of pepper to a large pan.
2. Leave for 5–7 minutes, or until soft. Increase the heat and wait for the liquid to boil before adding the tomatoes. Ten minutes of simmering at medium heat

should be enough to thicken the sauce. Set aside.

3. In a larger basin, combine the flour, remaining salt, and pepper. In a small dish, whisk the eggs and milk. Put the bread crumbs in a third medium bowl. First, dredge the eggplant slices in the flour mixture, then in the eggs, and last, in the breadcrumbs.

4. Oil should be heated for one minute in a big pan over medium heat. For a golden-brown finish, fry eggplant slices in batter for 1–2 minutes each side. Slices should be placed on a baking pan coated with paper towels.

5. A temperature of 350 degrees Fahrenheit should be set on the oven. One cup of tomato sauce should be served on the side. Put some tomato sauce in a big, deep baking dish. Layer some sliced eggplant on top.

6. Tomato sauce should be spread on top of the slices. Top the tomato sauce with the remaining 1/4 cup basil, 2 tablespoons of the Parmesan. Layer it on three more times. Top it all off with some sliced mozzarella.

7. To make sure the cheese is golden and bubbling, bake the dish in the middle of the oven for 25-30 minutes.

8. After 15 to 20 minutes, remove the dish from the oven and let it cool slightly before serving it with the warmed tomato sauce and the remaining fresh basil.

Dietary Composition: Caloric Intake: 350, Quantity of fat: 15g, Quantity of Carbohydrates: 35g, Quantity of Protein: 15g, Quantity of Fiber: 5g

141. Grilled Portobello Mushrooms

Readiness Time: 16 minutes Time needed to cook: 3-5 minutes Quantity of Meals: 6

Required Material:

- Mushrooms:
- Garlic: 3
- A drop of olive oil

- Black pepper, to taste; Kosher salt or gritty sea salt, to taste;

Step-By-Step Procedure:

1. Prepare a medium fire in the grill. Use moist paper towels to clean out the black membrane from the bottom of the cap of the mushrooms to get rid of any debris. Put the garlic!

2. Dip each mushroom in the oil, which has been seasoned with garlic, and place them on a rack to dry. Salt and pepper the mushrooms, then cook it until a fork can easily penetrate them.

3. Slice the bread and arrange it on plates for accompanied the mushrooms.

Dietary Composition: Caloric Intake: 42, Quantity of fat: 1g, Quantity of Carbohydrates: 7g, Quantity of Protein: 4g, Quantity of Fiber: 2g

142. Kidney Bean Casserole

Readiness Time: 17 minutes Time needed to cook: 30-45 minutes Quantity of Meals: 6

Required Material:

- Olive oil, one teaspoon's worth
- Celery: 1/4 bunch. A yellow onion.
- Romaine lettuce, finely cut: 1/2 head
- Carrot purée: one cup
- Simple Vegetable Stock: One Cup
- kidney beans: 1 cup
- Cooked barley: Half cup
- Oregano and chili: (each) half a teaspoon

- Sprigs of fresh thyme: 3
- Cracked black pepper for seasoning

Step-By-Step Procedure:

1. Prepare 325 degrees Fahrenheit in the oven.
2. Prepare a bread or casserole dish by oiling it. You can eat celery raw if you cut it up.
3. Use a blender to mix the carrot puree with the stock. Cover and bake for 30–45 minutes, until beans are tender and celery and onions are translucent and barley is tender.
4. Presented on a bed of chopped lettuce.

Dietary Composition: Caloric Intake: 300, Quantity of fat: 13g, Quantity of Carbohydrates: 30g, Quantity of Protein: 13g, Quantity of Fiber: 8g

143. Lemon Asparagus with Parmesan

Readiness Time: 14 minutes Time needed to cook: 3-4 minutes Quantity of Meals: 6

Required Material:

- Salt: half tsp
- Juice and zest lemon: one
- Asparagus: 1 and a quarter pound
- One clove of garlic
- Parsley: One-fourth cup
- Pure oil: Two tablespoons
- Melted margarine: a single Tbsp
- Cheddar cheese with Parmesan: 2 ounces

Step-By-Step Procedure:

1. Warm water and 1/2 teaspoon salt in a six-quart jar to boiling.
2. Use a vegetable peeler to remove the skin off the lower two creeps of the asparagus stalks. Cut stalks into 3-inch sections.
3. Boil asparagus for 3 minutes and drain. Put asparagus in a large bowl of ice water, drain.
4. Mix lemon zest, juice, garlic, olive oil, liquefied margarine, and salt. Throw the

mixture over the asparagus. Serve asparagus with long Parmesan strips.

Dietary Composition: Caloric Intake: 116, Quantity of fat: 5.5g, Quantity of Carbohydrates: 12g, Quantity of Protein: 6g, Quantity of Fiber: 2.5g

144. Lemony Broccoli and Olives

Readiness Time: 13-15 minutes Time needed to cook: 5 minutes Quantity of Meals: 6

Required Material:

- Broccoli: 1 1/2 pounds
- Oil: about 2 tablespoons'
- Dark olives, halved and pitted: 1/4 cup
- Minced garlic clove: two
- Zest and juice of a lemon.

Step-By-Step Procedure:

1. Bring a 6-quart pot of salted water to a boil. Chop the broccoli stalks into 1-inch pieces after they have been peeled with a vegetable peeler to remove any rough outer skin.
2. Blanch the stems for 2 minutes in hot water, then add the florets and cook for 1 more minute.
3. In a skillet that doesn't stick, heat the oil over medium heat. Broccoli, olives, and garlic should be added after 4 minutes of sautéing and cooked until soft.
4. Toss with squeezed lemon juice, serve.

Dietary Composition: Caloric Intake: 95, Quantity of fat: 4.5g, Quantity of Carbohydrates: 10g, Quantity of Protein: 4g, Quantity of Fiber: 1g

145. Lentil and Walnut Chili

Readiness Time: 15-17 minutes Time needed to cook: 30 minutes Quantity of Meals: 6

Required Material:

- Red lentils: 2 cups
- Walnuts: half cup

- Shallots: 2
- Garlic: 4
- Peppers, poblano: two
- Olive oil: 1 tbsp
- Basic Vegetable Stock: 1 1/2 Cups
- Raw tomato paste: 2 1/2 cups
- Fat-free, plain yogurt: half cup
- Cumin: a tsp
- Chili powder: 1 1/2 tablespoons
- Honey: a single Tbsp

Step-By-Step Procedure:

1. Loosen any stones from the lentils and spread them out in a single layer on a baking sheet.
2. Nuts should be chopped and shallots should be sliced. Prepare the dish by mincing garlic and peppers.
3. Oil should be heated over low to medium heat in a pot. One to two minutes in a hot pan will do for the shallots, garlic, and peppers.
4. Everything else (save the lentils and the yogurt) should be combined. Lentils should be soaked for an hour before being added to the pot to simmer for another half an hour. Prepare bowls. Serve with a dollop of yogurt on the side.

Dietary Composition: Caloric Intake: 350, Quantity of fat: 15g, Quantity of Carbohydrates: 40g, Quantity of Protein: 15g, Quantity of Fiber: 10g

146. **Lentil-Stuffed Peppers**

Readiness Time: 20-23 minutes Time needed to cook: 40 minutes Quantity of Meals: 6

Required Material:

- Vegetables (Carrots, Onion yellow, celery stalks): 2 of each
- Ssprigs oregano: six
- A tablespoon olive oil
- Basic vegetable stock: One mug plus 3 mug, divided

- Lentils: 3 cups
- Sweet peppers: 6
- Cheese type feta: 3 ounces
- Fresh-cracked black pepper

Step-By-Step Procedure:

1. Finely chop the onion and celery. Peel the carrots and cut them into little cubes. Keep the oregano sprigs' tips and discard the remainder of the leaves.
2. Oil should be heated over medium heat in a big pot. Vegetables, such as onions, carrots, and celery, should be sautéed for 5 minutes before adding the lentils and the vegetable stock. The lentils should be cooked for around 15–20 minutes in a simmering liquid.
3. Peppers should have their stems and seeds removed and their tops lopped off.
4. Cover and cook the peppers in a small saucepan with the vegetable stock for 10 minutes.
5. After combining, spoon the mixture into the peppers.
6. The peppers should be served with the jars' lids propped open and the oregano leaves saved for garnish.

Dietary Composition: Caloric Intake: 155, Quantity of fat: 1.7g, Quantity of Carbohydrates: 27.2g, Quantity of Protein: 9.2g, Quantity of Fiber: 6.9g

147. **Olive, Bell Pepper and Arugula Salsa**

Readiness Time: 15-19 minutes Time needed to cook: 7 minutes Serve 1 ½ cups

Required Material:

- Extra-virgin olive oil: 1.5 teaspoons
- Crushed fennel seeds: 1 teaspoon
- Diced Kalamata olives: 16
- Red and yellow sweet peppers:
- Pepper & sea salt
- Baby arugula, diced: 1/2 cup

Step-By-Step Procedure:

1. In a big nonstick pan, heat the extra-virgin olive oil over medium heat; add the fennel seeds and cook for 1 minute, turning often.
2. After 4 minutes of sautéing, add the bell peppers and stir to combine.
3. Mix the peppers, salt, and pepper together in a bowl, then add the olives and toss to combine. Let stand for at least 2 minutes, stirring regularly, so the flavors can combine.
4. Add arugula and let it wilt somewhat. Serve

Dietary Composition: Caloric Intake: 40, Quantity of fat: 3g, Quantity of Carbohydrates: 3g, Quantity of Protein: 1g, Quantity of Fiber: 1g

148.   Potato and Fennel Gratin

Readiness Time: 22 minutes Time needed to cook: 1 hour and 45 minutes Quantity of Meals: 10

Required Material:

- A tablespoon butter without salt
- Evo oil: a quarter cup
- sliced fennel: 4 cups
- A large onion
- Yukon gold potatoes: 4 or 5 large
- Heavy cream and whole milk: in equal proportions of 1 mug
- Thyme leaves: a single Tbsp
- 1 teaspoon salt, divided
- Pepper: 1/2 teaspoon, divided
- Gouda cheese: 2 1/2 cups (grated, divided)
- Bread crumbs: 1/2 mug

Step-By-Step Procedure:

1. Put the dish in a preheated oven at 400 degrees. In a big, deep baking dish, liberally distribute butter.
2. Heat the oil for 30 seconds in a big skillet over medium heat. Add some onions and fennel. Vegetables need around 15

minutes of cooking time to become soft. Set aside.

3. In a large bowl, combine the potatoes with the cream, milk, and thyme. Layer the bottom of a baking dish with a third of the potato slices (save the remaining slices and the cream/milk for later).
4. Sprinkle the potatoes with half a teaspoon of salt, a quarter of a teaspoon of pepper, and a cup of cheese, then top with the remaining fennel mixture.
5. Layers of potatoes, fennel, and cheese are repeated, and then the process is repeated with a final layer of potatoes.
6. Cover the gratin in the baking dish with cream or milk.
7. Smooth and compress the potatoes by pressing down gently with your fingers. Sprinkle the remaining cheese over the top in an equal layer. Dot the top with breadcrumbs.
8. After 90 minutes in the oven, the potatoes should be extremely soft and the gratin should be golden and bubbling on top.
9. The gratin should rest for 20 minutes before being sliced and served.

Dietary Composition: Caloric Intake: 200, Quantity of fat: 15g, Quantity of Carbohydrates: 25g, Quantity of Protein: 5g, Quantity of Fiber: 4g

149.   Ratatouille

Readiness Time: 16 minutes Time needed to cook: 1 hour and 30 minutes Quantity of Meals: 6

Required Material:

- Eggplant, zucchini squash, yellow squash: One of each
- Leek: 1/2
- A plum tomato
- Shallot: one
- Garlic: two
- Sprigs marjoram: 2 pepper
- kalamata olives: 1/4 cup
- Oil of olive: 1/2 teaspoon
- Basic vegetable stock: one cup

Step-By-Step Procedure:

1. Prepare the vegetables by cutting them into big pieces (eggplant, zucchini, yellow squash, leek, and tomato) and shredding the shallot and garlic (finely). Chop the olives and mince the marjoram.
2. Combine all ingredients in a saucepan and cook slowly for 1 1/2 hours. Summer and Winter Squash.
3. Yellow squash is also called "summer squash." Many people classify squash as either a summer or winter kind.
4. The skins of summer squashes are papery, and the seeds are mushy.
5. The seeds and skins of winter squashes are both quite tough.

Dietary Composition: Caloric Intake: 250, Quantity of fat: 15g, Quantity of Carbohydrates: 22g, Quantity of Fiber: 4g, Quantity of Protein: 6g

150. Sautéed Broccoli Rabe

Readiness Time: 15-18 minutes Time needed to cook: 10-13 minutes Quantity of Meals: 6

Required Material:

- Broccoli rabe: Two pounds
- Oil: about 2 tablespoons
- Prepare 4 garlic cloves.
- Red pepper flakes: 1/4 teaspoon
- Chicken broth: 1/2 cup

Step-By-Step Procedure:

1. Remove the leaves from the broccoli rabe stem and put them in storage. Cut off a three-inch chunk of the tail.
2. Sauté the broccoli rabe stalks, leaves, and garlic for three minutes over medium heat while the olive oil heats.
3. Cook, covered, at a low simmer for 10 minutes after adding the chicken stock and red pepper flakes. Serve.

Dietary Composition: Caloric Intake: 80, Quantity of fat: 5g, Quantity of Carbohydrates: 5g, Quantity of Protein: 3g, Quantity of Fiber: 2g

151. Sautéed Eggplant Tomatoes, Dark Olives

Readiness Time: 15-19 minutes Time needed to cook: 30 minutes Quantity of Meals: 6

Required Material:

- Olive oil: 2 tablespoons
- Garlic: 3, hacked
- A huge eggplant
- Oregano: A tablespoon
- Tomatoes: One 28-ounce can
- Kalamata olives, glue tomato: 1/4 cup (each)
- Wine vinegar: Two tbsp
- Water: 1 to 3 tablespoons
- New basil, cut daintily: 1 cup
- Salt and pepper to taste
- Ricotta: 1/4 cup

Step-By-Step Procedure:

1. Olive oil should be heated over medium heat in a large skillet. After 5 minutes, add the oregano and cook for another 5 minutes.
2. Reduce the heat to medium-low and stir in the tomatoes, olives, tomato paste, and red wine vinegar. Cook for 15 minutes covered, stirring occasionally, until the eggplant is soft. To help the eggplant soften and cook, you may add 1 tablespoon of water to the container at a time.
3. Stir with salt and pepper to taste and stir in the basil; simmer for 3 to 5 minutes. Spoon some of the ricotta onto a plate, and serve.

Dietary Composition: Caloric Intake: 200, Quantity of fat: 12g, Quantity of Carbohydrates: 20g, Quantity of Protein: 12g, Quantity of Fiber: 3g

152.   Stuffed Grape Leaves Dish

Readiness Time: 19 minutes Time needed to cook: 1 hour and 20 minutes Quantity of Meals: 8

Required Material:

- Fresh grape leaves: 30
- EVO oil: two TBSP + a tbsp for top
- 2 cups finely diced onion
- Brown rice, raisins, pistachios: One cup of each
- Tomato juice: two mugs
- Sea salt and pepper, to taste
- Mint: a cup
- Pomegranate molasses, to drizzle
- Parsley: a single mug
- lemon juice: ¼ cup
- A lemon, sliced

Step-By-Step Procedure:

1. Cooking grape leaves in a saucepan of boiling water for approximately 2 minutes before draining and setting them aside is recommended.
2. Olive oil, preferably extra-virgin, should be heated in a large skillet over medium heat. Toss in the onions and cook for another 10 minutes, or until they begin to turn golden.
3. When the water reaches a soft boil, stir in the rice and reduce the heat to medium-low and cover the pot. Rice should be cooked for 40 minutes, or until the water is absorbed and the grain is soft.
4. Once the rice has been removed from the fire, Raise the temperature to 350 degrees Fahrenheit on your oven's control panel.
5. Line the bottom of a 2-quart baking dish with grape leaves and grease the sides with extra-virgin olive oil.
6. Using paper towels, dry the leaves, and then fill them halfway with the rice mixture.
7. Cover the top of the rice with additional grape leaves and the rest of the rice.
8. Create a cover out of the leftover leaves, and then fold the sides over to secure it.
9. Cook in a preheated oven for 40 minutes, or until the dish is firm and dry and the grape leaves are colored, brushing with additional virgin olive oil halfway through.
10. Wet a knife and divide the dish into eight servings; put the pieces on plates and top with pomegranate molasses and lemon slices.

Dietary Composition: Caloric Intake: 160, Quantity of fat: 7g, Quantity of Carbohydrates: 18g, Quantity of Protein: 5g, Quantity of Fiber: 5g

153.   Stewed Artichokes with Beans

Readiness Time: 14 minutes Time needed to cook: 20 minutes Quantity of Meals: 4

Required Material:

- fava beans, shelled: 1 ½ pounds
- Juice of lemon: 3 tbsp.
- Water: 4 cups
- Baby artichokes: 24
- A lemon half, to rub artichokes
- Oil of type EVO: 2 tsp.
- Thyme and Parsley: Four springs of each
- Red and black pepper: half tsp
- A tsp. sea salt
- Garlic: 3

Step-By-Step Procedure:

1. A large dish containing water and ice should be set aside. Bring some water to a boil in a medium saucepan over high heat.
2. Add the fava beans to the blender and process for 30 seconds. Drain the beans after 5 minutes and drop them in cold water to stop the cooking process.
3. Fava beans should have their skins removed before they are used.
4. Put the lemon juice and 4 cups of water into a separate big bowl.
5. Remove the artichoke's stiff outer leaves and cut off any excess stems. Remove any excess fat or peels, then rub each

ingredient with half a lemon before adding to the water.

6. The best results come from using a sauté pan with extra virgin olive oil heated over medium heat until the oil is extremely hot but not smoking.
7. After 2 minutes, when the shallot is beginning to brown, add the garlic, red pepper flakes, sea salt, and black pepper and stir.
8. Add 1 cup of the lemon water mixture and the artichokes, parsley, and thyme, and cook on low. Keep submerged under cover for 14 minutes.
9. Add three more minutes of cooking time and serve as soon as the beans are done.

Dietary Composition: Caloric Intake: 150, Quantity of fat: 5g, Quantity of Carbohydrates: 20g, Quantity of Protein: 8g, Quantity of Fiber: 6g

154. <u>Tomato and Feta Stuffed Peppers</u>

Readiness Time: 13 minutes Time needed to cook: 40 minutes Quantity of Meals: 4

Required Material:

- Feta cheese, crumbled: two mugs
- Tomatoes: (3 big, ripe).
- Sweet peppers or banana peppers: Eight
- Salt: 1.5 tablespoons
- Oil of olive: Half a cup
- Oregano: one teaspoon

Step-By-Step Procedure:

1. Put the dish in the oven and preheat it to 400 degrees F.
2. Half-fill a standard-sized saucepan with water and set it on the stove to boil.
3. After adding the salt, return the water to a boil. After five or six minutes of simmering over medium heat, take the peppers from the water using a slotted spoon.
4. Run cold water over the peppers to cool them down. Air-dry the peppers.
5. Pepper should be placed on the table. Keep the pepper whole, but remove the stem and seeds (if desired).
6. Fill the pepper's cavity with feta cheese until it forms a thin, horizontal line.
7. Arrange tomato slices next to the feta. Try your best to seal in all of the filler. Carry on until all of the peppers have been used.
8. Place the peppers tightly in a shallow baking dish.
9. Add the remaining salt and oregano to the peppers, and then sprinkle a quarter cup of oil over the top. Cover with foil and bake for 20 minutes.
10. Remove the foil and continue baking, uncovered, for 5 minutes, or until the liquid has evaporated.
11. Drizzle the remaining oil over the peppers and serve immediately.

Dietary Composition: Caloric Intake: 242, Quantity of fat: 11g, Quantity of Carbohydrates: 16g, Quantity of Protein: 17g, Quantity of Fiber: 4g

155. <u>Vegan Bruschetta</u>

Readiness Time: 11 minutes Time needed to cook: 2-3 minutes Quantity of Meals: 12

Required Material:

- Basil: eight leaves
- Tomatoes: two
- Garlic: half a teaspoon
- Italian bread: 12 slices

Step-By-Step Procedure:

1. To make the topping, combine the ingredients and spread them out over the bread.
2. Toast at 375 degrees Fahrenheit for a few minutes, or until crisp. Enjoy!

Dietary Composition: Caloric Intake: 200, Quantity of fat: 10g, Quantity of Carbohydrates: 26g, Quantity of Protein: 4g, Quantity of Fiber: 2g

156. Zucchini Parmesan

Readiness Time: 17 minutes Time needed to cook: 25 minutes Quantity of Meals: 6

Required Material:

- Zucchini: three medium-sized
- Skim Milk: 1 Cup
- Whites of eggs: 2
- Mozzarella cheese: 6oz
- Tomato sauce: 2 cups
- Bread crumbs: Half cup and 1 teaspoon of olive oil.
- Cracked black pepper for seasoning.

Step-By-Step Procedure:

1. Put in the oven and heat it to 400 degrees.
2. Cube the zucchini to a size of half an inch. Milk and egg whites should be whisked together. Toss the baking sheet with the oil.
3. Before dunking the zucchini in the egg, shake off any extra bread crumbs. Place on baking sheet and bake for 10 to 15 minutes, or until zucchini is fork-tender.
4. Put the sauce in a large casserole or baking dish. Layer the dish with a single layer of zucchini, then the cheese, and finally the sauce.
5. Keep going until you've used up all the ingredients, then pop them in the oven for 5-10 minutes, or until the cheese is melted and starting to brown. Season with black pepper to taste and serve.

Dietary Composition: Caloric Intake: 140, Quantity of fat: 5g, Quantity of Carbohydrates: 8g, Quantity of Protein: 10g, Quantity of Fiber: 2g

157. Zucchini Pie with Herbs and Cheese

Readiness Time: 14 minutes Time needed to cook: 1 hour and 30 minutes Quantity of Meals: 12

Required Material:

- Pure olive oil: half cup
- Scallions: twelve
- Zucchinis: Three (diced) + one larger zucchini sliced thinly into rounds
- Salt: half tsp
- Eggs: 5
- Baking powder: one teaspoon
- Flour, self raising: one cup
- Feta cheese crumbles: 1 cup
- Greek yogurt, and kaseri cheese (or Gouda): 1 cup of each
- Paprika, sweet: 2 tablespoons
- Fresh dill, chopped (1 cup)
- Pepper: a pinch

Step-By-Step Procedure:

1. An internal temperature of 350 degrees Fahrenheit should be set on the oven. Put the oil in a big pan and heat it for 30 seconds over medium heat. Add the salt, zucchini cubes, and scallions. Vegetables need around 20 minutes of cooking time to soften and release half of their juices. Take a break and take the skive away from the fire.
2. Scramble the eggs for two minutes in a big bowl once they've been broken open. Blend in the baking powder and flour. Mix with some Greek yogurt. Combine the veggies and melted cheeses. Pepper, 1 1/2 teaspoons paprika, and the sugar should be combined.
3. To prepare, oil a large, deep baking dish and pour in the ingredients. Over the

veggies, scatter the remaining paprika and the zucchini strips.

4. The dish should be baked in the middle of the oven for one hour. 15 minutes of cooling time is recommended before slicing and serving the pie...

Dietary Composition: Caloric Intake: 230, Quantity of fat: 13g, Quantity of Carbohydrates: 20g, Quantity of Protein: 8g, Quantity of Fiber: 2g

RICE AND GRAINS

158. Basic Lentils and Spiced Rice

Readiness Time: 15-18 minutes Time needed to cook: 1 hour and 10 minutes Quantity of Meals: 8

Required Material:

- Legumes: 1 cup (dried) or 2 cups of canned lentils.
- Two cups, plus one and a half cups of water
- Basmati rice: 1/2 mug
- Oil: a single tbsp
- cumin powder: a half a teaspoon
- A small onion, sliced
- Cinnamon, Turmeric: 1/4 teaspoon of each
- Cilantro: half cup
- Salt: Half tsp

Step-By-Step Procedure:

1. In a two-quart stockpot, bring the dried lentils and two cups of water to a boil over medium heat.

2. To make tender, simmer on low heat for 30 minutes.
3. You should heat the olive oil in a pan over medium heat and sauté the onion for 5 minutes after washing the rice in a colander several times to eliminate extra starch.
4. Mix the rice with the onions and garlic and sauté for a split second.
5. Cook till the water is boiling and add the remaining spices (cumin, cinnamon, and turmeric).
6. Cover and simmer for 30 minutes, or until the rice is tender but still somewhat chewy.
7. Rice, lentils, cilantro, and salt should be blended together just before serving.

Dietary Composition: Caloric Intake: 425, Quantity of fat: 2.5g, Quantity of Carbohydrates: 78g, Quantity of Protein: 15g, Quantity of Fiber: 12g

159. Baked Coconut Rice

Readiness Time: 16 minutes Time needed to cook: 55 minutes Quantity of Meals: 4

Required Material:

- Coconut oil: one teaspoon's worth
- Brown jasmine rice: about 2 cups, uncooked;
- Salt: to taste
- Flakes of coconut, already toasted: half mug
- Fresh pineapple slices: Half a cup of
- Water: two cups
- Coconut milk: a can of 13.5 ounces

Step-By-Step Procedure:

1. The oven has to be preheated to 375 degrees F.
2. Coconut oil should be melted in an oven-safe 4-quart saucepan over medium heat. After rinsing the rice well in a mesh strainer, it should be roasted in the coconut oil for 5 minutes while being stirred periodically. It needs salt, coconut milk, and water. Prepare boiling water for the rice.
3. Use aluminum foil or a heavy lid to thoroughly cover the pot before putting it in the oven. It takes 35 minutes to bake.
4. Try a bite to make sure it's nearly mushy. Add another 1/4 cup of water and bake for 10 more minutes if it's still not tender. The rice is done cooking if you cover it and let it rest for 5 minutes.
5. When ready to serve, fluff the rice and sprinkle with toasted pine nuts, coconut flakes, and sliced almonds...

Dietary Composition: Caloric Intake: 216, Quantity of fat: 9g, Quantity of Carbohydrates: 30g, Quantity of Protein: 3g, Quantity of Fiber: 2g

160. Black Bean & Barley Vegetarian Burritos

Readiness Time: 13-15 minutes Time needed to cook: 5-7 minutes Quantity of Meals: 4-6

Required Material:

- Barley: A half cup of dry
- A Tbsp olive oil
- Onion: 1 single
- Garlic dried: a Tsp
- Cumin Powder and salt: 1/4 teaspoon of each
- Black beans: one 15-ounce can
- Whole wheat tortillas: Six
- Tomato paste: three Tbsp worth
- Carrot: !
- Sour cream, salsa, shredded cheddar, or avocado for dipping

Step-By-Step Procedure:

1. Prepare the barley for roasting as directed on the box.
2. Olive oil should be heated in a medium saucepan over medium heat while the barley is cooking.
3. Add the carrot, black beans, tomato paste, onion, garlic, pepper flakes, cumin, salt, and pepper flakes. Stirring periodically, combine and cook for approximately five minutes. Remove the mixture from the heat and gently mash it with a fork.
4. When the barley is done, arrange the tortillas on individual plates and divide the barley and black bean mixture into six equal portions, placing each portion in the center of a tortilla.

Dietary Composition: Caloric Intake: Caloric Intake: 200, Quantity of fat: 6g, Quantity of Carbohydrates: 30g, Quantity of Protein: 10g, Quantity of Fiber: 6g

161. Chickpeas with Spinach

Readiness Time: 8-10 minutes Time needed to cook: 5 minutes Quantity of Meals: 4

Required Material:

- A tablespoon of olive oil
- Onions: half
- Minced garlic cloves: 4
- Salt: half tsp
- frozen spinach leaves: 16 ounces
- Chickpea: can, 14.5 fluid ounces
- Powdered cumin: equivalent to 1/2 teaspoon
- Paprika: a quarter tsp

Step-By-Step Procedure:

1. The onion and garlic should be sautéed in the olive oil in a small saucepan for approximately 5 minutes, or until the onion is transparent.
2. Blend the spinach, cumin, paprika, salt, and chickpeas together.

3. Crush the beans with a wooden spoon while the sauce simmers on low heat.
4. Place in oven and cook until serving time. Take out of the oven.
5. Serve.

Dietary Composition: Caloric Intake: 552, Quantity of fat: 10g, Quantity of Carbohydrates: 94g, Quantity of Protein: 16g, Quantity of Fiber: 16g

162. Couscous with Tomatoes & Cucumbers

Readiness Time: 15 minutes + refrigerate for 2 hours' Time needed to cook: 0 minutes Quantity of Meals: 6

Required Material:

- Water: 2 mugs
- Couscous made with whole wheat: one cup,
- ground coriander: half tsp
- Roma or plum tomatoes, sliced: 2
- Perfectly grown and diced cucumber: one.
- Red onion, diced: just 1/2
- Can of chickpeas, drained and rinsed: 14.5 ounces
- Mint leaves: 1/2 cup
- Lime juice: 1/3 mug
- Oil: a single Tbsp

Step-By-Step Procedure:

1. In a medium saucepan, bring approximately an inch of water to a boil. After incorporating the couscous and the coriander, cover the pot and remove it from the heat.
2. After adding the liquid, let the couscous sit for about 15 minutes to absorb it completely.
3. Salad components like tomatoes, cucumbers, onions, chickpeas, and mint may be tossed with the cooked couscous in a big serving dish.

4. After covering, put in the fridge for at least two hours.

Dietary Composition: Caloric Intake: 350, Quantity of fat: 7g, Quantity of Carbohydrates: 70g, Quantity of Protein: 12g, Quantity of Fiber: 5g

163. Dark Beans with Tomatoes and Feta

Readiness Time: 15-17 minutes Time needed to cook: 0 minutes Quantity of Meals: 8

Required Material:

- Tomatoes, cut thinly: (four
- Beans: two 14.5-ounce cans
- Onions: half
- Dill, fresh: 1/4 cups
- One lemon's worth of extract
- Extra-Virgin Olive Oil: Two Tablespoons
- Feta cheese: a quarter mug
- Salt

Step-By-Step Procedure:

1. Combine everything in a serving dish, except the feta and salt.
2. Garnish with feta and salt just before serving.

Dietary Composition: Caloric Intake: 280, Quantity of fat: 15g, Quantity of Protein: 15g, Quantity of Carbohydrates: 25g, Quantity of Fiber: 8g

164. Falafel

Readiness Time: 14 minutes Time needed to cook: 3-4 minutes Quantity of Meals: 6

Required Material:

- Chickpeas: 14.5-ounce jars
- Big onion: half (
- Parsley, cilantro: (each) Two tablespoons
- Drops of red pepper: half to one teaspoon
- Minced garlic: four

- Powdered cumin seeds: one teaspoon
- Heating powder: 1 teaspoon
- Flour: 1/4 cup
- Oli: about 2 tablespoons'
- Cucumber yogurt sauce should be served on the side.

Step-By-Step Procedure:

1. Blend the chickpeas, onion, parsley, cilantro, salt, red pepper drops, garlic, and cumin in a food processor for 3 minutes, stopping to stir sometimes.
2. Mix flour and preparation powder. Remove the chickpea blend from the food processor, add the flour mixture, and form twelve 3-inch patties.
3. Warm a skillet for 1 minute. Add patties without crowding the container. Sauté the patties for 3–4 minutes per side until they have a beautiful outside.
4. Serve hot. Serve with 1–2 tbsp of tzatziki.

Dietary Composition: Caloric Intake: 150, Quantity of fat: 10g, Quantity of Carbohydrates: 20g, Quantity of Protein: 7g, Quantity of Fiber: 2g

165. Gluten-Free Coconut Granola

Readiness Time: 14 minutes Time needed to cook: 15-20 minutes Quantity of Meals: 4

Required Material:

- Gluten-free rolled oats: 3 cups
- Sweetened shredded coconut: 1/2 cup
- Kosher salt. 1/4 teaspoon
- Maple syrup: One-third cup
- Almonds: One-half cup and
- Cranberries.: just one mug
- Canola oil: One tablespoon

Step-By-Step Procedure:

1. The oven should be preheated at 325 degrees F.
2. Line up a very large piece of paper and put it away.

3. Combine the coconut, gluten-free oats, salt, maple syrup, and coconut oil in a large bowl and stir to combine.
4. Combine everything in a bowl and then spread it out on a baking sheet.
5. Prepare for 15–20 minutes, stirring periodically, until a golden brown.
6. Subtract heat to add chill. The almonds and dried cranberries should be mixed in after the mixture has cooled.
7. You may eat it immediately, or store it for up to two weeks in the fridge.

Dietary Composition: Caloric Intake: 300, Quantity of fat: 14g, Quantity of Carbohydrates: 33g, Quantity of Protein: 3g, Quantity of Fiber: 3g

166. Golden Pilaf

Readiness Time: 17 minutes Time needed to cook: 20 minutes Quantity of Meals: 6

Required Material:

- Oil: 2 teaspoons
- Onion: one
- Raisin, golden: a quarter cup
- Long-grain rice: Just one cup
- Turmeric: 1/2 teaspoon
- Cinnamon, cardamom: (each) 1/8 teaspoon
- Chicken or vegetable stock, reduced in sodium: 2 cups
- Parsley: 1/4 cup

Step-By-Step Procedure:

1. A saucepan should be used to warm the olive oil .. For three minutes, fry the onions and garlic.
2. The rice, spices, and a pinch of salt went into a hot pan for a minute. After adding the stock, bring the mixture to a boil before covering.
3. When the rice is done cooking, remove it from the heat and stir in the parsley. Simmer for 15 to 18 minutes, or until the liquid is absorbed.
4. Serve.

Dietary Composition: Caloric Intake: 400, Quantity of fat: 10g, Quantity of Carbohydrates: 60g, Quantity of Protein: 20g, Quantity of Fiber: 2g

167. Healthy Butternut Squash Grain Bowl

Readiness Time: 18-20 minutes Time needed to cook: 40 minutes Quantity of Meals: 4

Required Material:

- Butternut squash, diced: one cup
- A teaspoon of olive oil and maple syrup
- Cinnamon: 1/4 teaspoons
- cracked pepper:: 1/4 teaspoons
- Pecans: a quarter cup.
- Wild rice, cooked :1 cup of
- Spinach: Two cups
- A Honeycrisp apple
- Cranberry: One-fourth cup

Step-By-Step Procedure:

1. The oven should be preheated at 325 degrees F.
2. Line up a very large piece of paper and put it away.
3. Combine the coconut, gluten-free oats, salt, maple syrup, and coconut oil in a large bowl and stir to combine.
4. Combine everything in a bowl and then spread it out on a baking sheet.

5. Prepare for 15–20 minutes, stirring periodically, until a golden brown.
6. Subtract heat to add chill. The almonds and dried cranberries should be mixed in after the mixture has cooled.
7. You may eat it immediately, or store it for up to two weeks in the fridge.

Dietary Composition: Caloric Intake: 434, Quantity of fat: 10g, Quantity of Carbohydrates: 66g, Quantity of Protein: 11g, Quantity of Fiber: 11g

168. Lemon Orzo Pasta

Readiness Time: 1 hour and 14 minutes Time needed to cook: 10-12 minutes Quantity of Meals: 8

Required Material:

- Orzo: (1/2 lb.)
- Scallion greens: 4
- Plum tomatoes or Roma styles: four
- Cucumber, grown and cut: 1
- Lemon zest and juice to taste
- Olive oil and Feta cheese: use the same quantity of a quarter mug
- Salt, and some feta or cheddar

Step-By-Step Procedure:

1. Cook the orzo for the specified time (10-12 minutes) in a large pot of boiling water (approximately 4 quarts). Dump the orzo into a dish of ice water through a sieve.
2. In the meanwhile, set up a serving platter for the vegetables. In a small bowl, mix together the olive oil, lemon juice, and salt.
3. Blend the pasta and vegetables together, then combine with the lemon sauce. Serve chilled, with crumbled feta on top, and at least an hour after making.
4. Serve

Dietary Composition: Caloric Intake: 200, Quantity of fat: 2g, Quantity of Carbohydrates: 37g, Quantity of Protein: 7g, Quantity of Fiber: 2g

169. Lentil Portion

Readiness Time: 13-15 minutes Time needed to cook: 1 hour and 20 minutes Quantity of Meals: 8

Required Material:

- Lentils dried: One cup
- Water: two mugs
- Olive oil, the total amount is 1 tablespoon.
- Onion, medium, chopped: 1/2 cup
- One carrot, two garlic cloves
- Breadcrumbs: a half cup
- Eggs: two
- Low-sodium vegetable stock: One cup
- Tomato Paste: Two Tablespoons
- Coriander, pepper type black: half a teaspoon of each
- Chopped Parsley: (About Half an Ounce)
- Grated Cheese Parmesan: One-quarter Cup

Step-By-Step Procedure:

1. In a medium stockpot, cover with water, and place over medium heat to bring to a boil.
2. Reduce to a simmer and cook for 30 minutes, or until meat is cooked.
3. The lentils may be combined with a moderate crushing action that channels the plentiful fluids.
4. Get the broiler up to 400 degrees. Spray some cooking oil onto a 9-by-5-inch serving pan before using it.

5. For three minutes, in a small saucepan over medium heat, sauté the onion, carrot, and garlic in one tablespoon of olive oil.
6. Combine the onion combination, the remaining olive oil, the parsley, and the stale bread in a large bowl. Put the lentil mixture into the serving container.
7. Place in oven and bake for 40 minutes. After another 10 minutes in the oven, sprinkle over more Parmesan cheese and serve.
8. After 10 minutes, the lentils will have settled and are ready to be served.

Dietary Composition: Caloric Intake: 230, Quantity of fat: 1.5g, Quantity of Carbohydrates: 40g, Quantity of Protein: 13g, Quantity of Fiber: 8g

170. Maple Pumpkin Pie Buckwheat Groats

Readiness Time: 17 minutes Time needed to cook: 15-20 minutes Quantity of Meals: 4

Required Material:

- Wild buckwheat groats: 1/2 cup
- Beverage almond milk (no sugar): 2/3 cup
- Pumpkin Pie Spice: Half a Teaspoon
- Salt: tsp 1/8
- Vanilla extract: half a teaspoon
- 100% maple syrup: 4 tsp.

Step-By-Step Procedure:

1. The groats should be soaked in water in the refrigerator overnight.
2. The next day, empty the grain. The mucin in the wheat will make the grain stickier than normal. Flush it out and give it a good rinse.
3. A 2-quart sauce pan will do well for combining the oats, almond milk, pumpkin pie spice, and salt.
4. Cook, covered, over high heat until it boils, then lower the heat to keep it at a simmer for 4 minutes.

5. Remove the cover, increase the heat so that the liquid is just simmering, and continue cooking for two more minutes, stirring regularly.
6. Add the maple syrup and vanilla essence once you've removed the pan from the heat.
7. Serve.

Dietary Composition: Caloric Intake: 250, Quantity of fat: 8g, Quantity of Carbohydrates: 40g, Quantity of Protein: 5 Quantity of Fiber: 3-5g

171.   Mediterranean Orzo

Readiness Time: 10 Time needed to cook: 10-13 minutes Quantity of Meals: 8

Required Material:

- Extra-virgin olive oil: just a Tbsp
- Orzo pasta: (14 ounces)
- Julienne-cut tomatoes that have been marinated in oil: 8.5 oz
- Feta, chees: 4 ounces
- Provolone cheese: a quarter cup
- Green onions: eight
- Italian style dressing: One jar (16 oz)

Step-By-Step Procedure:

1. Bring a big pot of water to a boil and add 1 tablespoon of olive oil to the water. Boiling water is ideal for cooking pasta. Please drain and chill when is ready.
2. In a very large bowl, combine the pasta, sun-dried tomatoes, green onions, feta cheese, and provolone.
3. The top should be dressed using Italian dressing. Mix it up.

Dietary Composition: Caloric Intake: 350, Quantity of fat: 6g, Quantity of Carbohydrates: 60g, Quantity of Protein: 10g, Quantity of Fiber: 6g

172.   Mediterranean Quinoa Stuffed Peppers

Readiness Time: 10-12 minutes Time needed to cook: 20-25 minutes Quantity of Meals: 2-4

Required Material:

- Huge red peppers: 2
- Ready-to-eat quinoa: one mug
- Low-sodium chickpeas, cherry tomatoes (the same quantity of each): One cup
- Halved Pine nuts: Tbsp Two
- Black olives: 2 Tbsp
- A garlic clove
- White wine vinegar and oregano: 1 teaspoon (each)
- Parsley, chopped (optional)

Step-By-Step Procedure:

1. Bring oven temperature up to 350 degrees F.
2. Bell peppers should have their stems and seeds removed before they are halved lengthwise and placed on a baking pan either with parchment paper or a silicone baking mat.
3. Combine the remaining ingredients in a bowl, then transfer to the pepper halves using a spoon.
4. The peppers are done when they are soft but still have their form, usually after 20-25 minutes in the oven.
5. Take out of oven and garnish with parsley (optional) just before serving.

Dietary Composition: Caloric Intake: 300, Quantity of fat: 8g, Quantity of Carbohydrates: 40g, Quantity of Protein: 10g, Quantity of Fiber: 4g

173. Moroccan Couscous

Readiness Time: 20 minutes Time needed to cook: 3-5 minutes Quantity of Meals: 8

Required Material:

- Vegetable stock: 1 1/2 cups
- Dates: A third of a cup
- Zest and juice of 1 orange
- Dried, chopped apricots: A third of a cup
- Golden raisins: One-third of a mug
- Cinnamon: One-fourth of a teaspoon
- Cumin: 1/2 teaspoon
- Coriander: 1-quarter tsp
- Combine the ground ginger and turmeric in a half teaspoon.
- Dry couscous: 2 cups, plain or whole wheat
- Butter: a tbsp
- Toasted almond slivers: 1/2 cup
- Mint: One-fourth cup
- Please season with salt

Step-By-Step Procedure:

1. In a medium pot, come the stock to a boil. Put in the couscous, spices, orange juice, orange zest, dates, apricots, raisins, and dried fruit.
2. Remove the pan from the heat and cover it.
3. The couscous needs 15 minutes to soak up the liquid. If your couscous is too thick or too dry, just add a little water, cover it, and let it rest for five minutes.
4. Uncover, and stir in the butter when it has melted. Add the salt after mixing in the almonds and mint.

Dietary Composition: Caloric Intake: 175, Quantity of fat: 0g, Quantity of Carbohydrates: 36g, Quantity of Protein: 6g, Quantity of Fiber: 2g

174. Prepared Eggplant Parmesan & Linguini

Readiness Time: 13 minutes Time needed to cook: 18-20 minutes Quantity of Meals: 8

Required Material:

- Flour: equivalent to one cup
- Salt: 1 teaspoon
- Pepper extract: 1 tsp
- Eggs: 2
- Water: One-fourth of a cup
- Panko bread crumbs: Three cups
- Dry oregano: one teaspoon
- 2 standard eggplants
- Juice from 1/2 a lemon
- Olive oil: a quarter cup
- Four ounces of fresh mozzarella
- Linguini: One pound
- Marinara or red pepper sauce: Four cups

Step-By-Step Procedure:

1. Warm the stove to 400°F. Mix flour, salt, and pepper. In another separate bowl, whisk the eggs and water. In a third, combine the panko and oregano.
2. Remove the eggplant's stem and lowest section and make 1/2-inch long incisions. Stop sautéing by rubbing the chopped eggplant with the lemon wedge.
3. Dip the eggplant in flour, shake off the excess, then dip it in the egg mixture and panko. Repeat with the leftover eggplant.
4. Warm 1 tablespoon olive oil on medium-high in a large cast-iron Dutch burner or skillet. Brown the breaded eggplants in batches for 3 minutes per side.
5. Transfer to prepared sheet. Repeat with the remainder eggplant, using 1 tablespoon of olive oil each group. Top each eggplant with a thin slice of new mozzarella and heat for 15 minutes.
6. Boil 3 quarts of water and cook the linguini according to the package and channel. Distribute the linguini on 8 dishes, top

with 1/2 cup hot sauce, and add eggplant Parmesan. Serve

Dietary Composition: Caloric Intake: 400, Quantity of fat: 15g, Quantity of Carbohydrates: 40g, Quantity of Protein: 20g, Quantity of Fiber: 4g

175. Quinoa Salad with Watermelon and Feta

Readiness Time: 15 minutes + quinoa cooking package directions Time needed to cook: 10-15 minutes Quantity of Meals: 4

Required Material:

- Organic quinoa: 1 1/2 cups of Simple Truth's
- Apple cider vinegar: 3 tbsp.
- Lemon juice: about 2 Tbsp worth
- Chees, type Feta: 1/4 cup
- Watermelon, seedless: 1 1/2 cup
- Italian seasoning: 3 tablespoons
- Pure olive oil: half mug
- Fine grain salt, to taste

Step-By-Step Procedure:

1. Follow the package instructions for cooking quinoa. Remove the waste and flush with cold water.
2. Put the vinegar, lemon juice, and onion in a small jar or bowl and use it as a dressing. Stir the ingredients together and add the olive oil as though you were styling. Season to taste with salt and pepper.
3. In a medium bowl, combine the cooked quinoa, cheese, watermelon, parsley, and dill. Salt and pepper to taste, either cold or at room temperature.

Dietary Composition: Caloric Intake: 238, Quantity of fat: 10g, Quantity of Carbohydrates: 32g, Quantity of Protein: 8g, Quantity of Fiber: 4g

176. Shrimp Pasta, Kalamata Olives, Feta

Readiness Time: 13-15 minutes Time needed to cook: 10-12 minutes Quantity of Meals: 4

Required Material:

- The Kitchen's Stainless Steel Downpour
- Oil: 2 teaspoons
- Garlic cloves, minced: THREE
- red pepper drops: 1/2 tsp.
- Young artichoke hearts: two cups
- Kalamata olives: One-half cup
- White wine: 1 cup
- A pound of medium shrimp, deveined
- Holy messenger hair pasta: Half pound
- Basil: 1/4 cup
- Cheddar Feta: a quarter mug

Step-By-Step Procedure:

1. Three quarts of water should be brought to a full boil. In the meanwhile, heat the olive oil in a nonstick pan that has been sprayed with cooking water.
2. Hold off on serving until the garlic and pepper flakes have had some time to cook in.
3. Add the wine and shrimp after 3 minutes, and keep simmering until the shrimp are no longer translucent, another 4 minutes. Pasta should be boiled for 2–5 minutes in salted water, according to package directions.
4. In a large serving bowl, mix the cooked pasta with the shrimp sauce until it is well coated. Add feta and basil before serving.

Dietary Composition: Caloric Intake: 600, Quantity of fat: 25g, Quantity of Carbohydrates: 60g, Quantity of Protein: 30g, Quantity of Fiber: 4g

177. Warm Fava Beans with Feta

Readiness Time: 15-17 minutes Time needed to cook: 5-6 minutes Quantity of Meals: 4

Required Material:

- Grill protector for nonstick cookware
- Garlic: Two
- Canned fava beans (that have been drained and washed): 14.5 ounces
- Tomatoes: one (14.5 ounce) can, no salt added.
- Parsley: 1/4 cup
- Grated cheese (cheddar or feta): 1/4 cup

Step-By-Step Procedure:

1. Put a few drops of water into a skillet of moderate size. Put in the onions and garlic and sauté for a minute over medium heat.
2. The fava beans should be added after 3 minutes, and the tomatoes after 5 minutes. Parsley chiffonade and feta cheese on top, please.

Dietary Composition: Caloric Intake: 270, Quantity of fat: 13g, Quantity of Carbohydrates: 24g, Quantity of Protein: 13g, Quantity of Fiber: 8g

178. Wild Rice Pilaf

Readiness Time: 10-13 minutes Time needed to cook: 0 minutes Quantity of Meals: 8

Required Material:

- Wild rice and orzo: Two cups (each)
- Baby spinach: 2 mugs
- Kalamata olives, pitted: 1/4 mug
- Dill, parsley, oil: a quarter cup of each
- One lemon's juice
- Grape tomatoes, halved lengthwise: a single cup
- Salt & pepper to taste
- Feta: 2 ounces

Step-By-Step Procedure:

1. In a large bowl, toss together the brown rice, orzo, spinach, olives, dill, and olive oil. Toss to coat.
2. Add the tomatoes and parsley and mix gently; then season with salt and pepper and a squeeze of lemon. Add some cheese as a last touch, and then serve.

Dietary Composition: Caloric Intake: 200, Quantity of fat: 6g, Quantity of Carbohydrates: 32g, Quantity of Protein: 4g, Quantity of Fiber: 2g

DESSERTS

179. Apricot Pastry

Readiness Time: 16 minutes Time needed to cook: 30 minutes Quantity of Meals: 6

Required Material:

- Flour: One cup
- Olive oil: two teaspoons
- Water, ice: a tsp
- Apricots: Two cups
- Walnuts: half a cup
- Apricot jam: one-fourth cup
- Currants: half a cup
- Light brown sugar: one-fourth cup

Step-By-Step Procedure:

1. It's recommended to preheat the oven to 375 degrees F.
2. Make a dough out of the flour, olive oil, and cold water.
3. On a baking sheet, roll out the dough into a big square.
4. Put the apricots, nuts, currants, jam, and sugar into the centre, press the sides together to within an inch or two, and then fold back the corners to create a tiny aperture. 30-minute roasting time

Dietary Composition: Caloric Intake: 17, Quantity of fat: 0.2g, Quantity of Carbohydrates: 4g, Quantity of Protein: 0.5g, Quantity of Fiber: 1g

180. Blueberry Ravioli

Readiness Time: 10 minutes +1-hour in the freezer Time needed to cook: 6-8 minutes Quantity of Meals: 6

Required Material:

- All-purpose flour: 1 cup
- Whole wheat flour, and semolina: Half cup (1/4 of each)
- Exactly one egg
- Sugar, Granulated: 1/4 Cup
- A white egg
- Olive oil: 2 tbsp. with 1 tbsp. water.
- A pint of blueberries
- Sugar: 1/4 cup
- Lemon rind: 1 tsp. (grated)

Step-By-Step Procedure:

1. Mix the wet components (eggs, oil, and water) with the dry ones (flour, sugar, and salt) on low speed until everything is incorporated. Give the dough an hour in the fridge to rest.
2. Roll out the dough on a floured surface. Divide into 4-inch squares, fill each with a spoonful of blueberries, fold into a triangle, and press to seal.
3. Prepare a pot of boiling water using two liters. The recommended time for cooking ravioli is 6-8 minutes. Drain the mixture, then divide it among serving plates. Top with sugar and citrus zest before serving.

Dietary Composition: Caloric Intake: 300, Quantity of fat: 4g, Quantity of Protein: 10g,

Quantity of Carbohydrates: 48g, Quantity of Fiber: 2g

181. Cinnamon Almond Cake

Readiness Time: 10-13 minutes Time needed to cook: 45 minutes Quantity of Meals: 12

Required Material:

- A cup sugar
- Grated lemon rind: 1/4 teaspoon
- Egg: 6 yolks + 6 only whites
- Almonds: 1/2 pound
- Cinnamon: 1/2 tsp
- Heavy cream: half cup
- Granulated sugar: 1/4 teaspoon
- A teaspoon brandy
- Chopped almonds, for garnish

Step-By-Step Procedure:

1. Turn the oven temperature up to 375°F.
2. Sugar, butter, and egg whites should be whipped until fluffy. Add some ground almonds and cinnamon to the mix.
3. It's important to beat egg whites until they form firm peaks. The ground almonds should be combined with a few tablespoons of whites, and then the other ingredients should be folded in.
4. The recipe calls for two oiled 8-inch square baking dishes. Remove from heat and set aside to cool immediately.
5. Whip the cream with the sugar and brandy. Layer cake, then spread filling in between, on top, and around the edges. Sprinkle some chopped almonds on top.

Dietary Composition: Caloric Intake: 350, Quantity of fat: 20g, Quantity of Carbohydrates: 38g, Quantity of Protein: 8g, Quantity of Fiber: 3g

182. Cinnamon Rolls with Tahini and Honey

Readiness Time: 15 minutes + let the dough rise for 2 hours, plus 3 hours' Time needed to cook: 25-30 minutes Quantity of Meals: 16

Required Material:

- Whole milk, warm: a single cup
- Active dry yeast: 2 1/4 teaspoons
- Vegetable oil: 3 tablespoons
- All-purpose flour, divided: 3 1/4 cups
- Sugar: 1/2 cup
- A large egg
- Salt
- Golden brown sugar: Three-quarter cup
- Cinnamon: 2 tablespoons
- Tahini and honey: (used same proportion) 3/4 cup
- Lemon zest: a tsp
- Juice from lemon: 2 tablespoons
- Butter, without salt: 1/4 cup plus 1 tablespoon (room temperature, divided)

Step-By-Step Procedure:

1. In a large basin, combine the yeast with the heated milk. In order for the yeast to activate, the mixture has to sit for 7-10 minutes. Add 1 cup of flour, 1 egg, 1 teaspoon of salt, and 1 tablespoon of oil. Work the 2 cups of flour in by hand until a soft, non-sticky dough forms. The dough needs at least two hours to double in size after being covered and let to rise in a warm place.
2. In a separate dish, mix the brown sugar and cinnamon together and put it aside. Combine the tahini, honey, lemon zest, and lemon juice in a separate small bowl. Combine everything by stirring, then put away.
3. Grease a baking dish that measures 13 by 9 inches. After the dough has risen, place it on a floured surface and pound it down with your fist. Roll out the dough to a 9-

by-14-inch sheet. Use the remaining butter to cover the dough, leaving a 1/2-inch border all the way around. Coat the whole burger with the brown sugar mixture.

4. To make a cylinder, start rolling the dough from the longest end. Cut the dough into ten equal pieces, and spread them out in a baking dish with space to expand. Leave the rolls in a warm location for three hours, or until they have doubled in size and the pan is full, covered with a tea towel. Preheat the oven to 375 degrees F.

5. The rolls should be baked on the center rack for 20-25 minutes. The tahini poured on each roll individually.

6. You may either reheat the rolls or serve them at room temperature.

Dietary Composition: Caloric Intake: 420, Quantity of fat: 17g, Quantity of Carbohydrates: 61g, Quantity of Protein: 8g, Quantity of Fiber: 5g

183.   Créme Caramel

Readiness Time: 10 minutes + refrigerate for 8 hours or overunight Time needed to cook: 30 minutes Quantity of Meals: 12

Required Material:

- Big egg yolks: eight
- Vanilla: 2 tablespoons extract
- Whole milk: 5 ounces
- Eggs: Four
- Sugar: Two teaspoons
- Water: a quarter cup

Step-By-Step Procedure:

1. In preparation, preheat the oven to 450 degrees Fahrenheit. Milk has to be cooked in a medium saucepan over moderate heat until it steams but does not boil. Remove from heat and add vanilla.

2. In a large bowl, beat the eggs with 1 cup of sugar until pale and fluffy; then, beat in the milk. Keep adding milk a little at a time until the eggs have absorbed it all, then put aside to chill.

3. Get ready a dozen ramekins of the 3-inch kind. In a small, nonstick saucepan, bring the remaining sugar and water to a boil over medium heat. Reduce to medium heat. Swirl the pan instead of stirring the sugar. As the water evaporates, the sugar will brown and turn into caramel.

4. Sugar burns quickly, so keep your distance from the stove. When the sugar has reached a dark golden color, take the pan from the stove and divide the caramel evenly among the pumpkins. Wait for the caramel to set.

5. Evenly distribute the custard among the ramekins.

6. Prepare a big baking dish. Halfway fill the pan with boiling water and place the ramekins inside. For around 25-30 minutes, or until they have set.

7. Carefully take the ramekins out of the water. Pumpkins should be allowed to cool to room temperature before being refrigerated for at least 8 hours, ideally overnight.

8. After running a little knife along the rim of each ramekin, invert them over a dessert dish to release the Creme Caramel.

Dietary Composition: Caloric Intake: 150, Quantity of fat: 8g, Quantity of Carbohydrates: 18g, Quantity of Protein: 4g, Quantity of Fiber: 0g

184.   Cypriot Loukoumia

Readiness Time: 11 minutes Time needed to cook: 20 minutes Quantity of Meals: : approximately 20 pieces

Required Material:

- Butter: /2 cup
- Milk: 1 1/2
- Flour: 2-cups
- Sugar: 1/2 cup
- Single, beaten egg
- Baking powder: one teaspoon
- An Orange Marmalade: Half a Cup
- Almonds: 1 cup

- Water from an orange flower: 2 tablespoons
- Cinnamon, nutmeg: same proportion of 1/2 tsp

Step-By-Step Procedure:

1. An interior temperature of 350 degrees Fahrenheit should be set on the oven.
2. In a saucepan, melt the butter over medium heat. Stirring continually with a wooden spoon, add the flour gradually to avoid lumps.
3. Turn the heat down to medium and add the milk slowly while stirring frequently to avoid lumps as the mixture thickens.
4. Remove the pan from the heat after all the milk has been added, then whisk in the sugar, egg, and baking powder until the dough is smooth and consistent.
5. Mix together marmalade, almonds, orange blossom water, cinnamon, and nutmeg to make the filling.
6. To get a uniform banana peel thickness, lay out dough pieces on a floured surface.
7. Spread a little amount of filling onto the center of each disc.
8. Each disc should be folded in half over the filling to make a half-moon, and the edges should be pinched together to seal well.
9. Bake the cookies for 20 minutes on a sheet lined with parchment paper.
10. A thirty-minute wait is requested in advance of serving

Dietary Composition: Caloric Intake: 105, Quantity of fat: 0.2g, Quantity of Carbohydrates: 24.6g, Quantity of Protein: 0.9g, Quantity of Fiber: 1g

185. Citrus, Honey and Cinnamon

Readiness Time: 10-12 minutes Time needed to cook: 2 minutes Quantity of Meals: 4

Required Material:

- Orange blossom water: 2 teaspoons
- Oranges: 4

- Raw honey: 2 tbsp
- A cinnamon stick
- Walnuts: 2 1/2 tablespoons

Step-By-Step Procedure:

1. Remove the peels and slice the oranges into rounds.
2. In the meanwhile, heat the orange blossom water, honey, and cinnamon stick together in a heavy small pot. Over low heat, whisk gently for approximately 2 minutes, or until a simmer develops.
3. After the oranges and liquid have cooled, top them with chopped walnuts and the hot liquid. Assembled in the refrigerator and serve when is cold

Dietary Composition: Caloric Intake: 103, Quantity of fat: 0.3g, Quantity of Carbohydrates: 27g, Quantity of Protein: 1.5g, Quantity of Fiber: 3g

186. Figs with Brie and Port Wine Reduction

Readiness Time: 15-17 minutes Time needed to cook: 5 minutes Quantity of Meals: 6

Required Material:

- Butter, unsalted: One tablespoon
- Figs: 6.
- Port wine: Two mugs
- Brie Cheese: 12 ounces
- Sugar: 1-quarter cup

Step-By-Step Procedure:

1. In a saucepan of suitable size, reduce the wine by half while cooking it over medium heat. Remove from heat and whisk in the chilled butter.
2. Prepare two-ounce servings of Brie. Cut the figs in half lengthwise.
3. Before serving, a wine reduction is poured onto the dishes, sugar is sprinkled on top, and the figs and brie are placed artistically.

Dietary Composition: Caloric Intake: 467, Quantity of fat: 16.3g, Quantity of Carbohydrates: 57.3g, Quantity of Protein: 10.3g, Quantity of Fiber: 5.3g

187. Fresh Fruit and Meringue

Readiness Time: 15 minutes Time needed to cook: 5-6 hours Quantity of Meals: 12

Required Material:

- Egg whites: six
- Sugar: half a cup
- Tartar sauce: a quarter tsp
- Fresh fruit: 2 cups
- Grated lemon rind: a quarter tsp
- Almonds: 1/2 pound
- Honey: 3 Tablespoons

Step-By-Step Procedure:

1. Raise the oven temperature to a scorching 200 degrees F. Line or coat a baking sheet with parchment paper or cooking spray and set it aside.
2. In a bowl made of copper or stainless steel, beat the egg whites, sugar, and cream of tartar until they form firm peaks. A tablespoon at a time, sprinkle onto a baking sheet, and bake for 5-6 hours, or until dry, crispy, and faintly browned.
3. Serve with fruit that is currently in season. To add some shine, flavor with lemon zest, almonds, and honey.

Dietary Composition: Caloric Intake: 250, Quantity of fat: 5g, Quantity of Carbohydrates: 50g, Quantity of Protein: 5g, Quantity of Fiber: 3g

188. Fresh Fruit Chowder

Readiness Time: 16 minutes Time needed to cook: 0 minutes Quantity of Meals: 6

Required Material:

- Plum, Strawberry
- Blackberries: 1/2 cup
- Mint: Three leaves
- Pineapple, Diced canned: one cup
- Blueberries: A half cup
- Yogurt, fat-free plain: Three ounces
- Cocoa powder, 1/4 cup (if you prefer)

Step-By-Step Procedure:

1. Create peach and plum wedges. The strawberries should be halved. Reduce the blackberries by half. Remove the mint leaves off the stems and save the tips for decoration.
2. Puree the pineapple in a blender or food processor. Put the pineapple puree in a shallow basin and add the other fruits. Mint leaves, cocoa powder, and yogurt with a minty chocolate drizzle.

Dietary Composition: Caloric Intake: 250, Quantity of fat: 5g, Quantity of Carbohydrates: 45g, Quantity of Protein: 6g

189. Galatopita (Milk Pie)

Readiness Time: 13 minutes Time needed to cook: 1 hour. And 20 minutes Quantity of Meals: 6

Required Material:

- Milk: Five cups
- Butter: half mug
- Sugar and fine semolina: a cup of each
- Eggs: 3

- Sugar crystals or ground cinnamon (for decorate)

Step-By-Step Procedure:

1. A temperature of 350 degrees Fahrenheit should be set on the oven. Bring the milk close to a boil on the burner.
2. A thick cream may be made by combining butter, sugar, and semolina and continually stirring the mixture.
3. To rapidly cool anything, remove it from the heat and let it stand for a few minutes. Beat the eggs, then whisk them into the thickened mixture.
4. Butter or oil the interior and outside of a pie dish or other high-walled, even-heating pan. Bake for an hour, or until the top is browned, after pouring mixture into baking dish.
5. Leave the pie in the oven for an additional 15 minutes after turning off the heat.
6. The pie needs to rest for a few hours after you take it out of the oven. Sprinkle with cinnamon and confectioners' sugar before serving. To give it that extra something, spread on some of your favorite jam or fruit.

Dietary Composition: Caloric Intake: 450, Quantity of fat: 30g, Quantity of Carbohydrates: 30g, Quantity of Protein: 15g, Quantity of Fiber: 2g

190. Lemon-Coconut Ice Cream

Readiness Time: 15 minutes + refrigerate for 8 hours or overunight Time needed to cook: 0 minutes Quantity of Meals: 4

Required Material:

- Milk of coconut: 16 ounces
- Condensed milk: 10 oz
- Honey: 1/4 cup
- Fresh lemon juice: five tablespoons
- Vanilla essence: one tablespoon
- Salt: half a teaspoon
- Grated lemon zest: two teaspoons

- Yogurt, Greek: 1 1/2 mug
- Lightly toasted, sugared coconut flakes: A single cup

Step-By-Step Procedure:

1. Whisk together the yogurt, lemon zest, lemon juice, coconut milk, and condensed milk in a large bowl.
2. The combination should be chilled in the refrigerator for at least 8 hours, preferably overnight, after being wrapped in plastic.
3. Follow the ice cream maker's directions for mixing and freezing the cream.
4. After scooping the ice cream into a plastic container, place it in the freezer to harden.
5. Garnish it with toasted coconut flakes.

Dietary Composition: Caloric Intake: 200, Quantity of fat: 10g, Quantity of Carbohydrates: 24g, Quantity of Protein: 3g, Quantity of Fiber: 2g

191. Lemon Meringue Phyllo Tarts

Readiness Time: 26 minutes Time needed to cook: 10-15 minutes Quantity of Meals: 6

Required Material:

- Ground almonds: 1/4 cup;
- Unsalted butter: Five Tbsp (loosed) + 6 (cut cube)
- Sugar, 1/4 cups plus 2/3 cups.
- Sheets of phyllo pastry: 4 and
- Thawed big eggs (keep the egg whites in the fridge until ready to use): 6
- Salt: around 1/8 teaspoon
- Fresh lemon juice: 1/3 cups
- Grated lemon zest: two teaspoons
- Tartar cream: three-quarters of a teaspoon
- Sugar: a quarter mug

Step-By-Step Procedure:

1. Pre-heat the oven to 325 degrees Fahrenheit. In a separate dish, combine 1/4 cup sugar and 1/4 cup almonds; then, using a muffin tin and 1 tablespoon of

melted butter, process 6 cups of the mixture until it resembles fine crumbs. Do this fast so the phyllo doesn't dry up: spread a sheet out on your counter and massage it with the melted butter.

2. Sprinkle one-third of the sugar-almond mixture onto the button, then repeat with a second cookie and set it atop the first. Put a third layer on top of the second, and so on. After spreading butter on the fourth sheet, lay it buttered-side up on top of the third.

3. Cube the stick into 4x4 pieces. Squares should be baked in buttered muffin tins for 10 minutes, or until gently brown.

4. Take the phyllo cups out of the muffin tray after 5 minutes and let them to cool on a rack. One or two days before to use, the phyllo cups may be prepared and stored at room temperature.

5. Put the curd in a bowl of icy water. Put two inches of water into a medium pot and set it over low heat. In a medium metal basin, whisk together the egg yolks and the remaining sugar until light and fluffy.

6. Mix in the lemon juice, salt, and zest. The bowl should be heated in the water at a low temperature in a pan.

7. The curd should thicken as you stir in the cold butter, about 6 tablespoons at a time. The curd should be cooled quickly, so place the metal dish it is in on top of the ice bath.

8. After the curd has cooled to room temperature, refrigerate it overnight, stirring it periodically.

9. Place the egg whites in a clean mixing basin and beat them with a mixer on medium speed until soft peaks form. The tempo should begin slowly and gradually build to mild peaks.

10. Once the whites have been whipped to a glossy, silky consistency and can hold their shape when piped, the tartar cream and confectioners' sugar may be folded in. Meringue should be placed in a large-mouthed piping bag.

11. Set a phyllo cup on the counter and fill it with cooled lemon curd to make the appetizers. Then, meringue should be piped on top. Repeat with the remaining meringues and curd in separate cups, lightly toasting them each time with a kitchen blowtorch.

12. You may serve the tarts immediately, or you can put them in the fridge to save for later. Tarts should be served at room temperature.

Dietary Composition: Caloric Intake: 300, Quantity of fat: 10g, Quantity of Carbohydrates: 35g, Quantity of Protein: 3g, Quantity of Fiber: 2g

192.   Lemon Sorbet

Readiness Time: 10 minutes + freeze for 1 hour Time needed to cook: 0 minutes Quantity of Meals: 6-8

Required Material:

- Water: a single cup
- Sugar: 3-quarter mug
- Fresh lemon juice: 3-quarter cup

Step-By-Step Procedure:

1. Stir the sugar into the water using a whisk. To prevent sugar crystals from forming, stir well. The sugar water should be stored in a basin far from the stove.

2. Mix in the lemon juice, cover, and chill rapidly in the refrigerator.

3. Make sure to freeze the mixture for at least an hour after combining it.

4. The combined material should be refrozen until it can be handled.

5. Just before serving, break up the sorbet and combine it in anything other than a food processor.

Dictary Composition: Caloric Intake: 68, Quantity of fat: 0g, Quantity of Carbohydrates: 17g, Quantity of Fiber: 0g, Quantity of Protein: 0g

193.   Lime Tart

Readiness Time: 17 minutes Time needed to cook: 25 minutes Quantity of Meals: 6

Required Material:

Tart Crust

- Unsalted butter: 1/4 cup
- Oil of olive: a quarter cup
- Water: 1 tablespoon
- Whole-wheat flour: 1-quarter mug
- Flour, all-purpose: half cup

For Filling:

- limes
- eggs, beaten
- cornstarch: 2 tablespoons
- sugar: 1/2 cup (granulated)
- A cup water

Step-By-Step Procedure:

1. Pre-heat the oven to 375 degrees F.
2. Mix the butter and oil, then mix the flour with a dough hook at low speed (or by hand), adding water one spoonful at a time. Roll out the dough on a floured surface and place in a pie pan. Bake for 10 minutes.
3. To make the zest, juice the lime and grate the ginger. Mix all of the following ingredients together, then bring them to a low simmer in a medium-sized saucepan and stir constantly until the mixture reaches a thick consistency. After the first

15 minutes of additional baking, pour the lime mixture into the unbaked pie shell. Continue baking the pie.

Dietary Composition: Caloric Intake: 350, Quantity of fat: 20g, Quantity of Carbohydrates: 35g, Quantity of Protein: 4g, Quantity of Fiber: 2 g

194.   Melomakarona (Walnut Cookies)

Readiness Time: 15 minutes + cover dough and let it rest for 30 minutes Time needed to cook: 50 minutes Quantity of Meals: 20

Required Material:

- Sugar: 4 mugs
- Water: Four Cups
- Honey: 1 Tbsp + One cup
- Cinnamon: 1 stick
- Orange peel strip: 1
- Pure olive oil: half cup
- Unsalted butter: 1/4 cup
- Metaxa brandy: One-fourth cup
- Grated orange zest: One tbsp
- Three-quarters of a cup of orange juice
- Semolina flour: 1/4 cup
- Baking powder: 1 1/2 teaspoon
- Cinnamon: 4 teaspoons ground
- Ground cloves: 1 teaspoon
- Walnuts: 1 1/2 cup
- Brown sugar: 1/3 cup
- Baking soda: a quarter tsp
- Pastry flour: Three mugs

Step-By-Step Procedure:

1. Over medium heat, bring water, honey, the orange peel, and a cinnamon stick to a boil with sugar. For the next 10 minutes, cook on medium-low heat. Let there be a cooling of the room.
2. Add the brandy, remaining honey, and orange zest to the bowl of a stand mixer equipped with the dough hook attachment and mix on medium speed for 5 minutes. Orange juice and baking soda should be

combined in a small bowl. Once you've added everything to the mixer, mix for another minute.

3. In a large bowl, combine the two types of flour, the baking powder, the salt, two tablespoons of cinnamon, and half a teaspoon of cloves. Slowly, one cup at a time, pour the dry ingredients into the mixer. After all the ingredients have been combined, cover the bowl and let the dough rest for 30 minutes until it is soft and malleable but not sticky.

4. A temperature of 350 degrees Fahrenheit should be set on the oven. divide the dough into 40 equal pieces. Make an oval out of anything that was once round. To make a design on top of the cookie, gently press it on the fine side of a box grater. The cookie sheet should be lined with parchment paper before being inserted into the oven. Use the remaining balls in the same way.

5. Prepare a baking time of 30 minutes for the cookies. Drop the warm cookies into the reserved syrup a few at a time. Ten minutes in the syrup, flipped over for another three, please. Transfer the cookies to a rack to cool.

6. In a little bowl, combine the remaining walnuts with the brown sugar, cinnamon, and cloves. Spread the remaining syrup over the cookies, then top with the nut mixture. The cookies should be stored in an airtight container.

Dietary Composition: Caloric Intake: 150, Quantity of fat: 8g, Quantity of Carbohydrates: 18g, Quantity of Protein: 2g, Quantity of Fiber: 1g

195. Orange Crepes

Readiness Time: 14 minutes Time needed to cook: 3-4 minutes Quantity of Meals: 6

Required Material:

- Flour: 1/2 cup
- Eggs: 2 whole + 2 only whites
- Skim milk: 1/2 cup

- Orange juice fresh: 1 1/2 cups
- A teaspoon fresh orange zest, divided
- Butter: 1/2 teaspoon (melted)
- A teaspoon cold unsalted butter
- Sugar: 1/4 cup c

Step-By-Step Procedure:

1. Flour, eggs, milk, 1/4 cup orange juice, and 1/2 teaspoon orange zest should be mixed together until smooth.

2. Heat up a pan that can hold liquid, such a skillet or sauté pan. Combine the melted butter with the dry ingredients.

3. Flip the crepe over when the bubbles appear in the batter and the underside is a bright golden color. Just reheat in the microwave.

4. To make the orange syrup, bring the remaining orange juice to a boil in a small saucepan.

5. Reduce the juice by half by boiling it, then whisk in the cold butter.

6. The crepes should be served on a plate (or a field) and doused with the reduced juice before being sprinkled with the remaining zest and sugar.

Dietary Composition: Caloric Intake: 250, Quantity of fat: 9g, Quantity of Carbohydrates: 34g, Quantity of Protein: 7g, Quantity of Fiber: 2g

196. Pear Croustade

Readiness Time: 15 minutes + chill the dough for 1 hour Time needed to cook: 40 minutes Quantity of Meals: 8

Required Material:

- All-purpose flour: one cup plus one tablespoon.
- Sugar: Four + half Tbsp
- Salt: 1/8 tsp
- Butter, without salt: Six Tbsp
- A big egg
- Water, ice-cold: 1 1/2 tbsp
- Pears Bosc: 3

- Lemon, only juice: a tbsp
- Allspices ground: 1/3 tsp
- Anise (seed: a single tsp

Step-By-Step Procedure:

1. Pulse together 1 cup of flour, 1.5 teaspoons of sugar, and salt in a food processor. When you add the butter, pulse the mixture until it looks like coarse crumbs. Combine the components in a large bowl.
2. Separately, prepare a small basin with cold water and place the egg yolk in it. Blend the flour, butter, and egg mixture together by stirring. Roll out a small ball of dough and flatten it into a disc.
3. Refrigerate the dough for at least an hour after wrapping it in plastic.
4. Raising the oven temperature to 400 degrees Fahrenheit is a good idea. The dough should be rolled out to a circle approximately 10 inches in diameter.
5. Get the dough and baking sheet into the oven right away. In a large bowl, combine the pears with the rest of the sugar, the rest of the flour, the lemon juice, the allspice, and the anise.
6. Distribute the filling in an equal layer over the dough, leaving a 2-inch border all the way around. To make a ragged edge, fold the border of dough over the fruit. If there are any gaps in the dough, squeeze them shut.
7. In a separate bowl, whip the egg white with a whisk and then drizzle it over the dough.
8. The topping should be golden and bubbling after 40 minutes in the oven, at which point you should remove the baking sheet from the oven and allow it cool for 15 minutes before serving. Warm or room temperature is ideal for serving croustade.

Dietary Composition: Caloric Intake: 310, Quantity of fat: 18g, Quantity of Carbohydrates: 33g, Quantity of Protein: 3g, Quantity of Fiber: 4g

197.   **Pistachio and Fruits**

Readiness Time: 12 minutes Time needed to cook: 5-6 minutes Quantity of Meals: 12

Required Material:

- Fried pistachios: 1 1/4 cups
- Apricots: 1/2 cup (dried)
- Cranberries: A quarter cup
- Sugar: Two tsp
- Pinches of Cinnamon
- Allspice: 1/4 teaspoons
- Nutmeg: 1/4 teaspoon

Step-By-Step Procedure:

1. Put the pistachios on a baking sheet and bake them at 350 degrees Fahrenheit for about 6 minutes.
2. Get them out of the heat and into a cool place.
3. Mix everything in a dish and serve.

Dietary Composition: 150, Quantity of fat: 9g, Quantity of Carbohydrates: 14g, Quantity of Protein: 4g, Quantity of Fiber: 2g

198.   **Poached Apples**

Readiness Time: 9 minutes Time needed to cook: 30-45 minutes Quantity of Meals: 6

Required Material:

- Apples: Six
- A lemon
- Apple cider: a Cup
- White wine, sweet: a quarter mug
- Whole cloves: 3
- Cinnamon: half tsp
- Golden raisin: a quarter cup

Step-By-Step Procedure:

1. Take the core apples out. Zest and juice the lemon.

2. Apples should be fork-tender after being cooked in a covered pan for 30–45 minutes with sugar, wine, lemon juice, zest, cloves, and cinnamon. Stay cozy and have the apples ready.

3. The cooking liquid has to be reduced. Apples are served with a drizzle of raisin.

Dietary Composition: Caloric Intake: 44, Quantity of Carbohydrates:12g, Quantity of fat: 0g, Quantity of Protein: 0g, Quantity of Fiber: 2g

199. Rice Pudding

Readiness Time: 15 minutes + 8 hours in the refrigerator Time needed to cook: 1 hour and 30 minutes Quantity of Meals: 12

Required Material:

- Long grain rice: Two and a half cups
- Milk, whole: nine cups
- Cinnamon stick
- Salt: 3-quarter tsp
- Vanilla extract: a tbsp
- Lemon and orange strips: 6
- Sugar: a cup
- Egg yolks: 2
- Raisin: half cup
- Water, warm: a single cup
- Ground cinnamon, 1 tsp.

Step-By-Step Procedure:

1. In a large saucepan over medium heat, combine the rice with 8 cups of milk, the cinnamon stick, salt, the vanilla bean, the lemon peel, the orange peel, and the sugar. Maintain constant stirring until the milk is hot but not boiling. Drop the thermostat to medium-low immediately.

2. It takes approximately an hour and a half to cook rice until it's tender. The pudding has to be rich and smooth. Take off the cinnamon stick, citrus peels, and orange peel before serving, and remember to stir the rice every so often so it doesn't stick.

3. Scald the remaining milk (bring it to the point where it almost boils) in a small saucepan over medium heat.

4. Whisk the eggs in a small bowl until they are completely combined. Slowly add a ladleful of milk while whisking the eggs. Slowly add the milk, stirring constantly, until it has been completely absorbed by the eggs.

5. Let the raisin drain. Beat the eggs and add them to the rice pudding along with the raisin. Put the pudding in a casserole dish and set the temperature to room temperature. Refrigerate, covered, for at least 8 hours and up to overnight.

6. Put on some cinnamon and serve the rice pudding hot in the living room.

Dietary Composition: Caloric Intake: 250, Quantity of fat: 5g, Quantity of Carbohydrates: 45g, Quantity of Protein: 6g, Quantity of Fiber: 2g

200. Tiramisu

Readiness Time: 25 minutes + refrigerate it for 8 hours or overunight Time needed to cook: 0 minutes Quantity of Meals: 10

Required Material:

- Big eggs divided: 3
- Nutmeg: one-eighth of a teaspoon
- Mascarpone cheese: One cup
- Sugar: a quarter cup
- Freshly prepared, strong black coffee: One-half cup
- Ladyfinger biscuits: 16
- Cocoa powder: 2 tablespoons
- Marsala: or coffee liquor 6 tbsps

Step-By-Step Procedure:

1. In a medium bowl, whisk together the egg whites, nutmeg, and 2 tablespoons of sugar until stiff peaks form. Put there the mascarpone. In a second medium bowl, whip the egg whites until they hold firm peaks. The egg whites should be softly

folded into the mascarpone and egg mixture. Leave it be.

2. In a medium bowl, combine the remaining sugar, coffee, and marsala. Make sure the sugar is well dissolved by stirring the mixture. Soak eight ladyfingers in the coffee mixture for a count of one second, then lay in a serving dish. If you leave ladyfingers in coffee for longer than a nanosecond, they will get mushy.

3. The ladyfingers should have half of the mascarpone filling spread on them. Repeat with the remaining ladyfingers, dipping each one for 1 second in the coffee mixture before placing them above the filling in the serving dish. Cover the ladyfingers with the remaining mascarpone filling. Cover and chill the tiramisu in the fridge for at least 8 hours and up to overnight. Before serving, dust the dessert with chocolate powder. Cold or room temperature serving is recommended.

Dietary Composition: Caloric Intake: 489, Quantity of fat: 27g, Quantity of Carbohydrates: 42g, Quantity of Protein: 8g, Quantity of Fiber: 1g

CONCLUSION

The word "diet" conjures up images of deprivation, acute hunger, and tasteless, uninteresting meals as things we have to consume in order to lose weight; nevertheless, the Mediterranean diet is everything but those things.

In the Mediterranean diet, you may choose from a large choice of foods that are all fresh, nutritious, all natural, and all natural. Although some of the substances get more attention than others, none of the natural compounds are overlooked in the process.

Dieters who follow the Mediterranean eating plan may retain eating many of the traditional foods that are a part of their diet while also developing a deeper understanding for the positive effects that certain natural components can have on their health.

The eating patterns of the people who originally inhabited the beaches of Greece, Italy, Spain, Morocco, and France served as the primary source of motivation for the development of this diet. These regions are blessed with an abundance of seasonal fresh fruit, vegetables, and seafood due to the moderate temperature and location of the regions.

To get a handle on the fundamentals of the Mediterranean diet, all you have to do is picture yourself dining like it's the middle of summer all the time. When you are reminded of the meals that you loved the most while on vacation or at the beach, you can have a feeling that you've experienced it before. In point of fact, following a Mediterranean diet is never dull.

In spite of the fact that you will be providing your body with the very greatest nourishment possible by adhering to the Mediterranean diet, you can still take pleasure in the food that you eat while doing so.

When the food you eat gives you the impression that you are on a continuous vacation, jumping on the bandwagon of the latest culinary trend is not only simple but also exhilarating.

Made in United States
Troutdale, OR
07/02/2023

10930171R00075